Your Voice Is a **Warrior's War Trumpet** Full of Fire.™

Declaring the U.S. Constitution

OOK 1 IN THE KINGDOM DECLARATION SERIES™

Nathan Daniel Pietsch

PRAYER VIDEO :: WWW.BATTLEAxETV.COM

Book 1 in the *Kingdom Declaration Series*™
Declaring the U.S. Constitution

Copyright © 2023 by All Sufficient God Church and Nathan D. Pietsch
All rights reserved.

ISBN-13: 978-0-9765775-1-5

Editor: Lauri Homestead

NOTICE OF RIGHTS
This book is protected under the copyright laws of the United States of America and may not be copied or reprinted for commercial gain or profit. Any quotations or excepts taken from this book must receive prior written consent from All Sufficient God Church and/or Nathan D. Pietsch.

NOTICE OF LIABILITIES
The information in this book is distributed on an "as is" basis without warranty. While every precaution has been taken in the preparation of this book, neither the publisher nor the ministry shall have any liability to any person or entity with respect to any loss or damage caused or alleged to be caused directly or indirectly by the information contained in this book. All Sufficient God Church nor Nathan D. Pietsch assume any liability or responsibility for the use or misuse of this book.

BIBLICAL REFERENCES
All Scriptural references are taken from the New King James Version (NKJV) of the Bible unless otherwise mentioned.

New King James Version (NKJV)
Copyright © 1982 by Thomas Nelson, Inc.

PURCHASE INFORMATION
Declaring the U.S. Constitution is available at special discount rates for bulk purchase. To arrange bulk purchase for sales promotions, premiums, or fundraisers, please contact All Sufficient God Church at: www.AllSufficientGod.org

LEARN MORE OR SCHEDULE NATHAN D. PIETSCH FOR SPEAKING ENGAGEMENTS
To learn more about All Sufficient God Church and/or to schedule Nathan D. Pietsch for speaking engagements, please contact us at: www.AllSufficientGod.org.

DEDICATION

I would like to dedicate Book 1 in the *Kingdom Declaration Series™: Declaring the U.S. Constitution* to my Heavenly Father, my Lord and Savior Jesus Christ, and the Holy Spirit. Everything else is insignificant in comparison to Them.

Acknowledgments

I would like to thank my bride, Dawn, for letting me take the time to write this book. She has been faithful to follow me on this grand adventure with the Lord.

I also want to thank the multitudes of people who have helped me and Dawn with our ministry call.

Jon Courson (Applegate Christian Fellowship)

Kristina Waggoner

Angelo, Andrea, Adam, and Aaron LiVecchi (We See Jesus Ministries, WeSeeJesusMinistries.com)

Alan and Lisa Gluck

Bill and Carol Doyel (Living Better 50, LivingBetter50.com)

Francisco and Carla Reyes (3rd Watch Ministries, 3rdWatchMinistries.com)

Roy and Lorelei Harris (Whirlwind Ministries International)

Sherry Haydel (Sherry Haydel Limited, SherryHaydelLtd.com)

Uzoma Kingsley Akanador and Regina Bianca George (Worphan Charity Organization)

Kathleen Krohn

Myron and Lorie Ace

Rich, Kelley, and Kallee Salber

Bill and Diane Squire

Sharon Lawler

Joe and Jamie Martin

Will and Pam Abbott

Lawrence and Lindsay Elliott

Pastors Frank and Parris Bailey (Victory Church, VictoryChurchNola.com)

Jeremiah Omoto Fufeyin (Christ Mercyland Deliverance Ministry, ChristMercyland.org)

Clint and Faye Pietsch.

Contents

PREFACE — PAGE 17

The U.S. Constitution (17)
The Bill of Rights (18)
Amendments 11-27 (19)

INTRODUCTION — PAGE 21

How Far Has the USA Fallen? (25)
Mobilizing God's Army (28)
How to Use This Book (30)
    1787 Transcription (30)
    21st Century Modern Language (30)
    Kingdom Declarations™ (31)

THE PREAMBLE — PAGE 33

ARTICLE 1 — PAGE 39

§ Section 1: The Legislature (40)
§ Section 2: The House (42)
    Clause 1 (42)
    Clause 2 (43)
    Clause 3 (44)
    Clause 4 (47)

Clause 5 (48)
§ Section 3: The Senate (50)
    Clause 1 (50)
    Clause 2 (52)
    Clause 3 (54)
    Clause 4 (56)
    Clause 5 (57)
    Clause 6 (59)
    Clause 7 (61)
§ Section 4: Elections, Meetings (63)
    Clause 1 (63)
    Clause 2 (64)
§ Section 5: Membership, Rules (66)
    Clause 1 (66)
    Clause 2 (68)
    Clause 3 (69)
    Clause 4 (72)
§ Section 6: Compensation (74)
    Clause 1 (74)
    Clause 2 (77)
§ Section 7: Revenue Bills (79)
    Clause 1 (79)
    Clause 2 (81)
    Clause 3 (85)
§ Section 8: Powers of Congress (88)
    Clause 1 (88)
    Clause 2 (90)
    Clause 3 (91)
    Clause 4 (92)
    Clause 5 (94)
    Clause 6 (96)
    Clause 7 (97)
    Clause 8 (98)
    Clause 9 (100)

- Clause 10 (101)
- Clause 11 (102)
- Clause 12 (103)
- Clause 13 (105)
- Clause 14 (106)
- Clause 15 (106)
- Clause 16 (108)
- Clause 17 (111)
- Clause 18 (112)

§ Section 9: Limits on Congress (114)
- Clause 1 (114)
- Clause 2 (116)
- Clause 3 (117)
- Clause 4 (118)
- Clause 5 (119)
- Clause 6 (120)
- Clause 7 (121)
- Clause 8 (122)

§ Section 10: Powers Prohibited (124)
- Clause 1 (124)
- Clause 2 (127)
- Clause 3 (129)

ARTICLE 2 — PAGE 133

§ Section 1: The President (134)
- Clause 1 (134)
- Clause 2 (136)
- Clause 3 (138)
- Clause 4 (141)
- Clause 5 (142)
- Clause 6 (144)
- Clause 7 (146)
- Clause 8 (147)

§ Section 2: Civilian Power (150)
        Clause 1 (150)
        Clause 2 (152)
        Clause 3 (155)
§ Section 3: State of the Union (157)
§ Section 4: Disqualification (161)

ARTICLE 3   PAGE 165

§ Section 1: Judicial Powers (166)
§ Section 2: Trial by Jury (168)
        Clause 1 (168)
        Clause 2 (170)
        Clause 3 (172)
§ Section 3: Treason (174)
        Clause 1 (174)
        Clause 2 (176)

ARTICLE 4   PAGE 179

§ Section 1: Honoring Each State (180)
§ Section 2: State Citizens (182)
        Clause 1 (182)
        Clause 2 (183)
        Clause 3 (184)
§ Section 3: New States (186)
        Clause 1 (186)
        Clause 2 (187)
§ Section 4: Republic Government (189)

ARTICLE 5   PAGE 193

Article 6 — Page 199

- Clause 1 (200)
- Clause 2 (201)
- Clause 3 (203)

Article 7 — Page 207

Signatories — Page 211

About Nathan Pietsch — Page 216

Additional Resources — Page 218

Additional Books — Page 219

Connect with Nathan — Page 221

Sow Into This Ministry — Page 222

Schedule Nathan — Page 223

Forefathers' Blood — Page 224

Get Right With God — Page 226

Your Voice Is a

Full of Fire.

Preface

THE U.S. CONSTITUTION

Outside of the Holy Bible, the U.S. Constitution is the supreme law of the United States of America. It was created on September 17, 1787. The opening words of the U.S. Constitution State:

"We the People of the United States, in Order to form a more perfect Union, establish Justice, insure domestic Tranquility, provide for the common defense, promote the general Welfare, and secure the Blessings of Liberty to ourselves and our Posterity, do ordain and establish this Constitution for the United States of America."

In this writing, Book 1 in the *Kingdom Declaration Series™: Declaring the U.S. Constitution,* our focus will be on what the U.S. Constitution says and means in modern language.

As you read on, you will declare each part of the Constitution with power and authority. You can also pray along with Nathan in a video at www.BattleAxeTV.com.

THE BILL OF RIGHTS

The U.S. Constitution has been amended or modified in order to make a correction or improvement 27 times. The first 10 Amendments are known as the Bill of Rights. These Rights offer specific protections of individual liberty and justice. They guarantee the rights of freedom of speech, press, and religion. They also place restrictions on the powers of government within the U.S. States.

In Book 2 in the *Kingdom Declaration Series™: Declaring the Bill of Rights*, we examine the first ten amendments to the U.S. Constitution. You will be able to understand each amendment in modern English and make powerful declarations written for you to follow.

AMENDMENTS 11-27

The bulk of the remaining 17 amendments expand individual civil rights protections. They also address issues related to federal authority or modify government processes and procedures. To learn more about Amendments 11-27 look at Book 3 in the *Kingdom Declaration Series™: Declaring Amendments 11-27*.

Introduction

We are living in uncertain times. Injustice seems to be prevailing. Parents are being bullied and sued for asking the educational board in their school district what their children are being taught. Law-abiding gun owners are termed evil for standing on their right to own a firearm. Villains are being heralded as heroes and heroes villains.

Leftist liberals want to abolish the U.S. Constitution. They claim it is nothing but a White Supremacist document that holds no relevance for today.

The United States is under attack. Its founding documents are being scrutinized. The constitutional federal republic is being threatened. Those who love America are at risk.

The battle against good and evil, moral and immoral, light and dark, right and wrong continues to rage. In recent days the intensity of evil has heightened. However, we shouldn't be surprised at this. Jesus warned us about such situations in John 16:1-4 when He said:

> [1] "These things I have spoken to you, that you should not be made to stumble. [2] They will put you out of the synagogues; yes, the time is coming that whoever kills you will think that he offers God service. [3] And these things they will do to you because they have not known the Father nor Me. [4] But these things I have told you, that when the time comes, you may remember that I told you of them."

We are in a spiritual war. The Apostle Paul wrote in Ephesians 6:12:

> [12] For we do not wrestle against flesh and blood, but against principalities, against powers, against the rulers of the darkness of this age, against spiritual hosts of wickedness in the heavenly places.

The true enemy against our freedoms, rights, nation, and lives are not people per se, but satanic entities controlling them. Fortunately, the Heavenly Father, Jesus, and Holy Spirit has given His children the ability to fight back in the spirit. We are told in 2 Corinthians 10:4:

> ⁴ *For the weapons of our warfare are not carnal but mighty in God for pulling down strongholds.*

As followers of Jesus Christ we have been empowered to pull down satanic strongholds warring against us. One way to pull down these strongholds, and perhaps the most powerful weapon of war the Lord has given you, is your voice. Your voice is a *Warrior's War Trumpet™* that destroys the works of the devil. Your voice sounds the alarm of danger. Your voice rallies the troops. Your voice carries fire. Your voice holds life and death. The Bible tells us in Proverbs 18:21:

> ²¹ *Death and life are in the power of the tongue, And those who love it will eat its fruit.*

There is a verse in Job that emphasizes the power of your words and declarations. The Bible says in Job 22:28a-b:

> ²⁸ *You [people] will also declare a thing, And it will be established for you...*

This is the significance of the *Kingdom Declaration Series™*. As you speak forth the declarations in this book, you will be co-creating and establishing dominion with God. Even if you do not understand the meaning behind the various Articles, Sections, and Clauses found in the Constitution, continue to speak forth the *Kingdom Declarations™*. Your words have power and your declarations will be established.

As you proclaim, let God put His holy fire in your mouth. Let your words be released with power and authority. The Book of James 5:16d says:

> ^{16d} *...The effective, fervent prayer of a righteous man avails much.*

HOW FAR HAS THE USA FALLEN?

The Constitution of the United States of America is our most significant national document. It was written by God-fearing men who followed the Bible. The Constitution was inspired, but it is not Holy Scripture. The ultimate document, and law of the land, is the Holy Bible.

However, as you go through this book, you will see how far America has fallen away from both the U.S. Constitution and Holy Bible. It is shocking to know how far off course our nation has veered. It is alarming to see how many unconstitutional and illegal laws are in effect today.

As you proclaim the declarations found in this book, you will help bring realignment to our nation. You will also be educated on what the Constitution says. You will be empowered to bring national transformation by using the authority of your voice.

We are at a critical point pertaining to the future of America. If the USA falls to the satanic agenda, so will the rest of the world. Americans need to be in a place of humility before the Lord, praying for mercy. We also need to be in a place of action.

The declarations in this book will thrust you into motion as you contend for the United States. It will also help you shift from a place of murmuring, complaining, and frustration into practical application.

As I previously mentioned, the U.S. Constitution will never replace the Holy Bible as the standard to live by. However, there are some lessons we can take from the Bible and compare that to the Constitution.

In the Book of 2 Kings 22, King Josiah ordered the renovation of the House of the Lord. During this process, a book of the law was discovered. These were the instructions God had given to His people through Moses. However, the people had fallen so far away from the governing instructions that their most sacred document was lost in the House of the Lord (2 Kings 22:5-8).

When the law was discovered and read to King Josiah, he humbled himself before God and tore his clothes (2 Kings 22:11). When Josiah realized how far the nation had fallen, his heart was broken and he wept. God saw Josiah's humility and honored him for it (2 Kings 22:19-20).

The opposite situation occurred in the Book of Jeremiah chapter 36. The Prophet Jeremiah wrote instructions, directions, and corrections to Israel, Judah, and all the nations (Jeremiah 36:2). Jeremiah's document might have been similar to the U.S. Constitution.

However, King Jehoiakim of Judah and his servants did not heed the instructions. They were not afraid, did not humble themselves, nor tear their clothes. Instead of following God's ordained directions given to Prophet Jeremiah, the king burned the document in the fire (Jeremiah 36:23-24).

The United States is in a similar situation as the people were in ancient days. We have fallen away from both Biblical principles and the U.S. Constitution. The USA is at the crossroad. Which way will we go? Will we follow King Josiah's example and turn the nation back towards God's desire, or will we be like King Jehoiakim who forsook the instructions, directions, and corrections of the land and burned the document in the fire?

MOBILIZING GOD'S ARMY

The devil's plan is to destroy all the nations of the world and America is in his cross hairs. His desire is to raise up people to fulfill his leftist agenda. The devil wants people to hate the Holy Bible, the U.S. Constitution, America, and anything pro-God.

However, until our time on this earth is expired and our spirits leave our bodies, we have an active role to play in combating satanic strategies. We must not sit back and watch our nation be destroyed.

God is calling you to arise and shine (Isaiah 60:1). God has set you aside for such a time as this (Esther 4:14). God is pouring out His extraordinary boldness on you (Acts 4:29-31). God is raising you to be strong and of good courage (Joshua 1:9). God is calling you to be a person of great valor (Judges 6:12). God is putting His Holy Spirit and fire on your voice (Acts 2:1-4). God is mobilizing you into His great army (Joel 2:11).

Declaring the U.S. Constitution, *Declaring the Bill of Rights*, and *Declaring Amendments 11-27* are weapons in your hand. They are tools to help prepare and organize God's army. They are explosions in the enemy's camp. They are signal fires to stir people into action. They are compasses to help realign our nation. They are battering rams destroying satan's plans.

As God mobilizes you into His army, pray how you can be used for His glory. Be sensitive to what the Lord might place on your heart. Listen to what He might whisper into your ears. Are you being called to lead your family through the declarations found in the *Kingdom Declaration Series™*? What about leading your church or small group? What about leading stadiums of people through these declarations as we contend for the future of the United States?

How to Use This Book

The entire U.S. Constitution contained in this book are broken into three different sections.

1787 Transcription

First, you will see the 1787 exact transcription of the U.S. Constitution. It is transcribed with the word usage and spelling as the original text written in 1787. You will find grammatical variances in comparison to our current language.

21st Century Modern Language

Second, you will see the U.S. Constitution written in 21st century modern language. This will make it easier for you to understand the meaning of the Constitution.

KINGDOM DECLARATIONS™

Third, you will see the U.S. Constitution broken down into a *Kingdom Declaration™*. In this section you will speak forth the prayers written for you. Each declaration will be proclaimed out loud. Verbalize the words with vigor in the name of Jesus Christ. If you like, you can follow along with Nathan as he leads you through the prayers in a video.

Please visit: www.BattleAxeTV.com.

The Preamble

1787 Transcription

We the People of the United States, in Order to form a more perfect Union, establish Justice, insure domestic Tranquility, provide for the common defence, promote the general Welfare, and secure the Blessings of Liberty to ourselves and our Posterity, do ordain and establish this Constitution for the United States of America.

21st Century Modern Language

We the people of the United States have made this Constitution for numerous reasons.

First, we want to make our union of the U.S. States better and stronger.

Second, we want to establish justice for all the citizens of the United States of America.

Third, we want the people and the various States to have a tranquil relationship and get along peacefully.

Fourth, we want to defend the States against all enemies domestic or foreign.

Fifth, we want to make the United States a good place to live. A place of health, happiness, and fortunes of people.

Sixth, we want to be sure that we and the generations to come will always enjoy the blessings of freedom.

That's why we [the authors of the U.S. Constitution] have agreed to this Constitution for the United States of America.

 KINGDOM DECLARATION™

In the name of Jesus Christ, on behalf of the United States of America, I declare the U.S. Constitution will make the unity between the States better and stronger.

In the name of Jesus Christ, on behalf of the United States of America, I declare justice will be established for all the citizens of the United States.

In the name of Jesus Christ, on behalf of the United States of America, I declare the people and the various States will have a tranquil relationship and get along peacefully.

In the name of Jesus Christ, on behalf of the United States of America, I declare we will defend the United States against all enemies both domestic and foreign.

In the name of Jesus Christ, on behalf of the United States of America, I declare the United States is a good place to live.

In the name of Jesus Christ, on behalf of the United States of America, I declare the United States is a place of health and happiness for people.

In the name of Jesus Christ, on behalf of the United States of America, I declare the United States is a place where fortunes can be made.

In the name of Jesus Christ, on behalf of the United States of America, I declare my generation and future generations will always enjoy the blessings of freedom.

§ Section 1: The Legislature

1787 Transcription

All legislative Powers herein granted shall be vested in a Congress of the United States, which shall consist of a Senate and House of Representatives.

21st Century Modern Language

This Constitution gives Congress the power to make laws for the United States. Congress will be composed of two parts: A Senate and a House of Representatives.

Kingdom Declaration™

In the name of Jesus Christ, on behalf of the United States of America, I declare Godly men and women will be in Congress.

In the name of Jesus Christ, on behalf of the United States of America, I declare the laws made by Congress will reflect the values and morals of the Holy Bible.

In the name of Jesus Christ, on behalf of the United States of America, I declare those who make up the Senate and House of Representatives will be hand picked by the Heavenly Father, Jesus, and Holy Spirit.

§ Section 2: The House

Clause 1

1787 Transcription

The House of Representatives shall be composed of Members chosen every second Year by the People of the several States, and the Electors in each State shall have the Qualifications requisite for Electors of the most numerous Branch of the State Legislature.

21st Century Modern Language

The members who make up the House of Representatives shall be elected every two years. The residents of the various U.S. States shall elect the members of the House of Representatives.

Kingdom Declaration™

In the name of Jesus Christ, on behalf of the United States of America, I declare the members of the House of Representatives are elected every two years, not more and not less.

Article 1 -43-

In the name of Jesus Christ, on behalf of the United States of America, I declare the residents of the various U.S. States shall elect the members of the House of Representatives.

CLAUSE 2

1787 TRANSCRIPTION

No Person shall be a Representative who shall not have attained to the Age of twenty five Years, and been seven Years a Citizen of the United States, and who shall not, when elected, be an Inhabitant of that State in which he shall be chosen.

21ST CENTURY MODERN LANGUAGE

A Representative to Congress must be a minimum of 25 years old. He must also be a U.S. citizen for more than seven years. Finally, he must live or be a resident in the State that elects him.

KINGDOM DECLARATION™

In the name of Jesus Christ, on behalf of the United States of America, I declare each member of Congress and future Representatives are at least 25 years old.

In the name of Jesus Christ, on behalf of the United States of America, I declare those elected into Congress will be U.S. citizens longer than seven years.

In the name of Jesus Christ, on behalf of the United States of America, I declare those who are elected into Congress will live or be a resident of the State that elects him.

CLAUSE 3

 1787 TRANSCRIPTION

Representatives and direct Taxes shall be apportioned among the several States which may be included within this Union, according to their respective Numbers, which shall be determined by adding to the whole Number of free Persons, including those bound to Service for a Term of Years, and excluding Indians not taxed, three fifths of all other Persons.

The actual Enumeration shall be made within three Years after the first Meeting of the Congress of the United States, and within every subsequent Term of ten Years, in such Manner as they shall by Law direct. The Number of Representatives shall not exceed one for every thirty Thousand, but each State shall have at Least one Representative; and until such enumeration shall be made, the State of New Hampshire shall be entitled to choose three, Massachusetts eight, Rhode-Island and Providence Plantations one, Connecticut five, New-York six, New Jersey four, Pennsylvania eight, Delaware one, Maryland six, Virginia ten, North Carolina five, South Carolina five, and Georgia three.

21ST CENTURY MODERN LANGUAGE

U.S. States that have a larger population will have more Representatives. As a result, they will pay larger sums of taxes to the government.

We will determine how many Representatives a State will have in the following way. 1.) We will count all of the free people (non slaves). 2.) Then we will add three fifths of the number of people who are slaves. 3.) This will then determine the amount of taxes each State will pay.

People who are bound to service for a term of years are also included in the category of "free people." They are only temporary servants and need to be counted. However, this does not include Native Americans who don't get taxed. (Note: This was modified by the 14th Amendment. Check out Book 3 in the *Kingdom Declaration Series*™: *Declaring*

Amendments 11-27.)

After the first Congress meets, people will be counted within three years. Following the first counting, people will be counted every ten years. Congress will determine how the census shall be conducted.

For every 30,000 people, there will be one Representative. Even if a State does not have such a population they will still have at least one Representative.

Until each census is complete and the number of people is known, these States will have the following number of Representatives:

New Hampshire: 3

Massachusetts: 8

Rhode Island and Providence Plantations: 1

Connecticut: 5

New York: 6

New Jersey: 4

Pennsylvania: 8

Delaware: 1

Maryland: 6

Virginia: 10

North Carolina: 5

South Carolina: 5

Georgia: 3

KINGDOM DECLARATION™

In the name of Jesus Christ, on behalf of the United States of America, I declare the U.S. States with a larger population density will have more representation.

In the name of Jesus Christ, on behalf of the United States of America, I declare taxes paid to the federal government will be used in ways that glorify the Lord.

In the name of Jesus Christ, on behalf of the United States of America, I declare censuses done by Congress will be true and accurate.

CLAUSE 4

 1787 TRANSCRIPTION

When vacancies happen in the Representation from any State, the Executive Authority thereof shall issue Writs of Election to fill such Vacancies.

21st Century Modern Language

When a vacancy occurs in representation, the Executive Authority (governor) shall call for an election. A vacancy might happen due to death, forced removal, or resignation. At this occurrence, the people shall elect a new Representative.

 ### Kingdom Declaration™

In the name of Jesus Christ, on behalf of the United States of America, I declare when a vacancy in representation occurs, the governor of my State will conduct a true and fair election to fill the open position with a Godly and moral person.

Clause 5

 ### 1787 Transcription

The House of Representatives shall chuse their Speaker and other Officers; and shall have the sole Power of Impeachment.

21ST CENTURY MODERN LANGUAGE

The members in the House of Representatives will choose a leader. Their leader is known as, "Speaker." They will also choose other officers. Only the individuals in the House of Representatives may impeach or remove one of their members.

KINGDOM DECLARATION™

In the name of Jesus Christ, on behalf of the United States of America, I declare the members in the House of Representatives will choose a Godly Speaker of the House.

In the name of Jesus Christ, on behalf of the United States of America, I declare the Speaker will have Biblical morals, values, and convictions.

In the name of Jesus Christ, on behalf of the United States of America, I declare other officers chosen will have a Godly perspective on how to lead.

In the name of Jesus Christ, on behalf of the United States of America, I declare all Representatives that are doing fraudulent or unlawful acts will be exposed and immediately removed from their position.

Declaring the U.S. Constitution

§ SECTION 3: THE SENATE

CLAUSE 1

1787 TRANSCRIPTION

The Senate of the United States shall be composed of two Senators from each State, chosen by the Legislature thereof, for six Years; and each Senator shall have one Vote.

21ST CENTURY MODERN LANGUAGE

The Senate of the United States will have two Senators from each State. The legislatures from the individual States will chose their Senators. The Senators will be in office for six years. (The 17th Amendment implemented a change to the time limit of six years. See Book 3 in the *Kingdom Declaration Series™: Declaring Amendments 11-27*.)

Each Senator shall have one vote.

KINGDOM DECLARATION™

In the name of Jesus Christ, on behalf of the United States of America, I declare the Senate of the United States will have two Senators that represent each State.

In the name of Jesus Christ, on behalf of the United States of America, I declare each Senator will have an encounter with Jesus that transforms their lives.

In the name of Jesus Christ, on behalf of the United States of America, I declare the Senators will follow the Lord with their whole hearts.

In the name of Jesus Christ, on behalf of the United States of America, I declare an outpouring of the Holy Spirit in the Senate.

In the name of Jesus Christ, on behalf of the United States of America, I declare the legislatures from each State will choose God-loving and God-fearing Senators.

In the name of Jesus Christ, on behalf of the United States of America, I declare each Senator will have one vote that they cast in alignment with the Heavenly Father, Jesus, and Holy Spirit.

Clause 2

1787 Transcription

Immediately after they shall be assembled in Consequence of the first Election, they shall be divided as equally as may be into three Classes. The Seats of the Senators of the first Class shall be vacated at the Expiration of the second Year, of the second Class at the Expiration of the fourth Year, and of the third Class at the Expiration of the sixth Year, so that one third may be chosen every second Year; and if Vacancies happen by Resignation, or otherwise, during the Recess of the Legislature of any State, the Executive thereof may make temporary Appointments until the next Meeting of the Legislature, which shall then fill such Vacancies.

21st Century Modern Language

After the first group of Senators are elected, they will be split into three separate groups. They will be divided as equally as possible.

The first group of Senators will serve two years. The second group of Senators will serve four years. The third group of Senators will serve the full six years. By doing it this way, in every two years one third of all the Senators will be chosen. After the first initial groups of Senators, all future Senators will be elected for the full six year term.

If a Senator dies, resigns, or is removed, the State's legislature will pick a new Senator. If the legislature is not meeting, the Executive (governor) may choose a person as a temporary Senator. When the legislatures gather again, it can elect a new Senator at this time. (The 17th Amendment implemented a change to the time limit of six years. See Book 3 in the *Kingdom Declaration Series™: Declaring Amendments 11-27.*)

KINGDOM DECLARATION™

In the name of Jesus Christ, on behalf of the United States of America, I declare Godly Senators will enter the Senate.

In the name of Jesus Christ, on behalf of the United States of America, I declare all Senators with an anti-Christ agenda will be removed.

In the name of Jesus Christ, on behalf of the United States of America, I declare all vacant Senator seats will be filled with God's anointed and chosen vessels.

In the name of Jesus Christ, on behalf of the United States of America, I declare all temporary Senators will have an immediate impact that helps shift the Senate towards the Heavenly Father, Jesus, and Holy Spirit.

In the name of Jesus Christ, on behalf of the United States of America, I declare the legislatures will elect new Senators who carry God's values, morals, and wisdom.

CLAUSE 3

 1787 TRANSCRIPTION

No Person shall be a Senator who shall not have attained to the Age of thirty Years, and been nine Years a Citizen of the United States, and who shall not, when elected, be an Inhabitant of that State for which he shall be chosen.

21st Century Modern Language

In order to become a Senator, the candidate must be at least 30 years of age. He must be a U.S. citizen for a minimum of nine years. He must also live in or be a resident of the State where he is elected Senator.

Kingdom Declaration™

In the name of Jesus Christ, on behalf of the United States of America, I declare the Lord will elect the Senators He desires to represent the people.

In the name of Jesus Christ, on behalf of the United States of America, I declare God's elected Senators will have supernatural wisdom.

In the name of Jesus Christ, on behalf of the United States of America, I declare the elected Senators will have an unconditional love for America.

In the name of Jesus Christ, on behalf of the United States of America, I declare the elected Senators that need to be removed will be removed immediately.

In the name of Jesus Christ, on behalf of the United States of America, I declare the elected Senators will represent God, their States, and the people well.

Clause 4

 1787 Transcription

The Vice President of the United States shall be President of the Senate, but shall have no Vote, unless they be equally divided.

 21st Century Modern Language

The Vice President of the United States shall be President of the Senate. The President of the Senate will not be allowed to vote. However, he will be allowed to vote in the event a tied vote needs to be broken.

 Kingdom Declaration™

In the name of Jesus Christ, on behalf of the United States of America, I declare the Vice President of the United States will be a sold out lover of the Heavenly Father, Jesus, and Holy Spirit.

In the name of Jesus Christ, on behalf of the United States of America, I declare if the President of the Senate ever needs to vote, the person will vote for truth and righteousness.

Clause 5

1787 Transcription

The Senate shall chuse their other Officers, and also a President pro tempore, in the Absence of the Vice President, or when he shall exercise the Office of President of the United States.

21st Century Modern Language

The Senate should choose other officers. If the Vice President is not there, the Senate should choose another person to be in charge of the meetings. The person chosen is called President pro tempore, because it is only for a time. The President pro tempore will be in charge over the Senate when the Vice President is not there. The President pro tempore will also preside over the Senate if the Vice President is acting as or has become the President of the United States.

Kingdom Declaration™

In the name of Jesus Christ, on behalf of the United States of America, I declare the Senate will choose officers that reflect the morals and values found in the Holy Bible.

In the name of Jesus Christ, on behalf of the United States of America, I declare all people chosen to be in charge of meetings will be ordained by the Heavenly Father, Jesus, and Holy Spirit.

In the name of Jesus Christ, on behalf of the United States of America, I declare all President pro tempores will exude characteristics that reflect heaven.

In the name of Jesus Christ, on behalf of the United States of America, I declare if the Vice President ever becomes President of the United States the Vice President will lead the nation into repentance and turn towards God.

CLAUSE 6

1787 TRANSCRIPTION

The Senate shall have the sole Power to try all Impeachments. When sitting for that Purpose, they shall be on Oath or Affirmation. When the President of the United States is tried, the Chief Justice shall preside: And no Person shall be convicted without the Concurrence of two thirds of the Members present.

21ST CENTURY MODERN LANGUAGE

The Senate has the full power to try all impeachments. (This would include impeachments of the President, Vice President, Congress people, judges, and the like.) If Senators are trying an impeachment, they will be under oath. This means they are obligated to be truthful and precise.

If the President of the United States is in the process of impeachment, the Chief Justice will be in charge of the Senate. In order to convict a person of impeachment, two thirds of the Senators in attendance must be in agreement.

Kingdom Declaration™

In the name of Jesus Christ, on behalf of the United States of America, I declare incoming and future Senators will have a heart to do what is right and fair.

In the name of Jesus Christ, on behalf of the United States of America, I declare all evil doers in politics will be exposed of their crimes and be held accountable within the full extent of the law.

In the name of Jesus Christ, on behalf of the United States of America, I declare all politicians and judges who need to be impeached, let that process begin now.

In the name of Jesus Christ, on behalf of the United States of America, I declare all Senators trying an impeachment will be honest under oath.

In the name of Jesus Christ, on behalf of the United States of America, I declare if the President of the United States is evil, let him be impeached and held accountable for his crimes within the full extent of the law.

In the name of Jesus Christ, on behalf of the United States of America, I declare the Chief Justice will be a person of heavenly integrity.

Article 1 -61-

In the name of Jesus Christ, on behalf of the United States of America, I declare two thirds of the Senators must be present and in agreement in order to impeach a person.

In the name of Jesus Christ, on behalf of the United States of America, I declare there will not be mock or false trials or judgments.

CLAUSE 7

 1787 TRANSCRIPTION

Judgment in Cases of Impeachment shall not extend further than to removal from Office, and disqualification to hold and enjoy any Office of honor, Trust or Profit under the United States: but the Party convicted shall nevertheless be liable and subject to Indictment, Trial, Judgment and Punishment, according to Law.

 21ST CENTURY MODERN LANGUAGE

If a person is convicted in an impeachment trial they can only suffer the following consequences. First, remove the person from their job position. Second, their right to be elected to all other offices of honor must be taken away. Third, they can no longer work for the government.

If a person is convicted by the Senate, they may also be indicted, tried, judged, and punished according to the full measure of the law.

 KINGDOM DECLARATION™

In the name of Jesus Christ, on behalf of the United States of America, I declare if a person is impeached they will be removed from their job position.

In the name of Jesus Christ, on behalf of the United States of America, I declare if a person is impeached their right to be elected to all other offices of honor will be taken away.

In the name of Jesus Christ, on behalf of the United States of America, I declare if a person is impeached they can no longer work for the government.

In the name of Jesus Christ, on behalf of the United States of America, I declare all false accusations against God's anointed officials must stop now.

In the name of Jesus Christ, on behalf of the United States of America, I declare if a person is impeached and they are truly guilty they will be indicted, tried, judged, and punished to the full measure of the law.

§ SECTION 4: ELECTIONS, MEETINGS

CLAUSE 1

1787 TRANSCRIPTION

The Times, Places and Manner of holding Elections for Senators and Representatives, shall be prescribed in each State by the Legislature thereof; but the Congress may at any time by Law make or alter such Regulations, except as to the Places of chusing Senators.

21ST CENTURY MODERN LANGUAGE

The legislatures in each State will determine where, when, and how to conduct elections for the Senators and Representatives. However, at any time Congress can change where, when, and how to conduct elections for the Senators and Representatives. Congress cannot change the place where Senators are chosen.

KINGDOM DECLARATION™

In the name of Jesus Christ, on behalf of the United States of America, I declare Godly legislatures to represent each State.

In the name of Jesus Christ, on behalf of the United States of America, I declare God will give the legislatures wisdom on where, when, and how to conduct elections for Senators and Representatives.

In the name of Jesus Christ, on behalf of the United States of America, I declare there will be honest and fair elections.

In the name of Jesus Christ, on behalf of the United States of America, I declare God's chosen vessels will make up the U.S Congress.

CLAUSE 2

 1787 TRANSCRIPTION

The Congress shall assemble at least once in every Year, and such Meeting shall be on the first Monday in December, unless they shall by Law appoint a different Day.

21ST CENTURY MODERN LANGUAGE

All members of Congress must meet at least one day per year. The designated day is the first Monday in December. However, if they desire to choose a different day, they can. (Clause 2 was modified by the 20th Amendment. See Book 3 in the *Kingdom Declaration Series™: Declaring Amendments 11-27*.)

KINGDOM DECLARATION™

In the name of Jesus Christ, on behalf of the United States of America, I declare when Congress members meet, they will discuss ways to improve the United States.

In the name of Jesus Christ, on behalf of the United States of America, I declare the improvements will be inspired by the Heavenly Father, Jesus, and Holy Spirit.

In the name of Jesus Christ, on behalf of the United States of America, I declare the improvements will be implemented speedily and reflect the Kingdom of God.

§ Section 5: Membership, Rules

Clause 1

1787 Transcription

Each House shall be the Judge of the Elections, Returns and Qualifications of its own Members, and a Majority of each shall constitute a Quorum to do Business; but a smaller Number may adjourn from day to day, and may be authorized to compel the Attendance of absent Members, in such Manner, and under such Penalties as each House may provide.

21st Century Modern Language

The House of Representatives shall act as judge and determine if their own members are qualified. The House will also decide if they have been properly elected.

For a law to pass or to conduct business, more than half of the members in the House of Representatives must be in attendance. Other members can do a favor for absent members to come to the meeting. Each House can set up their own consequences for the people who do not come to work.

KINGDOM DECLARATION™

In the name of Jesus Christ, on behalf of the United States of America, I declare a holiness move in the House of Representatives.

In the name of Jesus Christ, on behalf of the United States of America, I declare the House will have keen discernment on determining if their members are qualified to represent U.S. citizens and Biblical morality.

In the name of Jesus Christ, on behalf of the United States of America, I declare the people elected will be elected properly and honestly.

In the name of Jesus Christ, on behalf of the United States of America, I declare fair and true elections.

In the name of Jesus Christ, on behalf of the United States of America, I declare for laws to pass and business to be conducted, more than half of the members will be in attendance.

In the name of Jesus Christ, on behalf of the United States of America, I declare the light of Jesus to shine into all dark areas of government.

In the name of Jesus Christ, on behalf of the United States of America, I declare the members in the House of Representatives will whole-heartedly invest in doing their job with the utmost integrity.

In the name of Jesus Christ, on behalf of the United States of America, I declare there will be right and just consequences for the people who do not act with integrity.

In the name of Jesus Christ, on behalf of the United States of America, I declare there will be right and just consequences for the people who refuse to come to work.

CLAUSE 2

1787 TRANSCRIPTION

Each House may determine the Rules of its Proceedings, punish its Members for disorderly Behaviour, and, with the Concurrence of two thirds, expel a Member.

21ST CENTURY MODERN LANGUAGE

Each House can determine how they conduct business. The House can determine their own rules for behavior and punish the members who do not follow the rules of behavior. If members do not oblige to the rules of behavior, they can be expelled from the House by a two thirds vote from the other members.

Kingdom Declaration™

In the name of Jesus Christ, on behalf of the United States of America, I declare each House will conduct business that represents the Heavenly Father, Jesus, and Holy Spirit.

In the name of Jesus Christ, on behalf of the United States of America, I declare the House rules for behavior will be in alignment with the Holy Scriptures.

In the name of Jesus Christ, on behalf of the United States of America, I declare members that do not follow the rules will be punished swiftly.

In the name of Jesus Christ, on behalf of the United States of America, I declare House members who refuse to honor God's Kingdom principles will be removed.

Clause 3

1787 Transcription

Each House shall keep a Journal of its Proceedings, and from time to time publish the same, excepting such Parts as may in their Judgment require Secrecy; and the Yeas and Nays of the Members of either House on any question shall, at the Desire of one fifth of those Present, be entered on the Journal.

21st Century Modern Language

Each House shall keep a journal or written record of the work conducted. This includes the laws that they pass. From time to time these records will be published and made known to the public.

However, there may be some parts that need to remain secret. If one out of five members desire to write down everyone's vote, then each member's vote will be recorded in the journal. The member's vote of "Yea" (yes) or "Nay" (no) will be written in the journal.

 ## Kingdom Declaration™

In the name of Jesus Christ, on behalf of the United States of America, I declare the journals in each House will be accurate and precise.

In the name of Jesus Christ, on behalf of the United States of America, I declare the laws they pass will be recorded in the journal.

In the name of Jesus Christ, on behalf of the United States of America, I declare the laws they pass will be ordained by the Heavenly Father, Jesus, and Holy Spirit.

In the name of Jesus Christ, on behalf of the United States of America, I declare the records will be published and made known to the public.

In the name of Jesus Christ, on behalf of the United States of America, I declare any law that is attempted to be passed that does not align with the will of God will be immediately stopped.

In the name of Jesus Christ, on behalf of the United States of America, I declare evil secrets that need to be exposed will come into the light of Jesus.

In the name of Jesus Christ, on behalf of the United States of America, I declare each member's vote will have God's stamp of approval.

In the name of Jesus Christ, on behalf of the United States of America, I declare all members who desire to vote against the good of the people will be swiftly removed.

CLAUSE 4

1787 TRANSCRIPTION

Neither House, during the Session of Congress, shall, without the Consent of the other, adjourn for more than three days, nor to any other Place than that in which the two Houses shall be sitting.

21ST CENTURY MODERN LANGUAGE

If Congress is in session, then one House may not take time off from work for more than three days. However, this delay will be permitted if the other House gives permission. In addition, Houses will be forbidden to meet where they don't usually meet unless permission is granted by the other House.

KINGDOM DECLARATION™

In the name of Jesus Christ, on behalf of the United States of America, I declare the Houses may not be in recess for more than three days if Congress is in session.

In the name of Jesus Christ, on behalf of the United States of America, I declare this delay may be permitted if the other House gives permission.

In the name of Jesus Christ, on behalf of the United States of America, I declare Houses will not meet where they don't usually meet unless permission is granted by the other House.

§ Section 6: Compensation

Clause 1

1787 Transcription

The Senators and Representatives shall receive a Compensation for their Services, to be ascertained by Law, and paid out of the Treasury of the United States. They shall in all Cases, except Treason, Felony and Breach of the Peace, be privileged from Arrest during their Attendance at the Session of their respective Houses, and in going to and returning from the same; and for any Speech or Debate in either House, they shall not be questioned in any other Place.

21st Century Modern Language

Senators and Representatives shall receive wages for the work they do. Members will vote on how much the Senators and Representatives will be paid. After the amount has been determined, the finances will come from the United States Treasury.

While Congress is in session, Senators and Representatives cannot be arrested. Nor can they be arrested going to or returning from their House of Congress. However, if they have committed treason, felony, or a breach of the peace then they can be arrested while in session.

If Senators or Representatives have given a speech or debate, they may not be questioned or arrested in either House. Nor shall they be questioned about their speech or debate in any other location.

 Kingdom Declaration™

In the name of Jesus Christ, on behalf of the United States of America, I declare Senators and Representatives will receive an honest and just wage.

In the name of Jesus Christ, on behalf of the United States of America, I declare all votes cast to determine pay salaries will be true and accurate.

In the name of Jesus Christ, on behalf of the United States of America, I declare the United States will have an abundance of finances.

In the name of Jesus Christ, on behalf of the United States of America, I declare the resources in the United States Treasury will be washed of evil in the blood of Jesus.

In the name of Jesus Christ, on behalf of the United States of America, I declare money circulating in the United States will be from honest and clean sources.

In the name of Jesus Christ, on behalf of the United States of America, I declare that money used for evil, and its sources, will be revealed and removed.

In the name of Jesus Christ, on behalf of the United States of America, I declare Senators and Representatives will not commit treason, felony, or breach of the peace.

In the name of Jesus Christ, on behalf of the United States of America, I declare Senators and Representatives have a heart and desire to follow the Heavenly Father, Jesus, and Holy Spirit.

In the name of Jesus Christ, on behalf of the United States of America, I declare speeches and debates given by Senators and Representatives will be ordained and anointed by God.

In the name of Jesus Christ, on behalf of the United States of America, I declare after Senators and Representatives give Holy Spirit inspired speeches and debates they will not be mocked, persecuted, or questioned.

CLAUSE 2

 1787 TRANSCRIPTION

No Senator or Representative shall, during the Time for which he was elected, be appointed to any civil Office under the Authority of the United States, which shall have been created, or the Emoluments whereof shall have been encreased during such time; and no Person holding any Office under the United States, shall be a Member of either House during his Continuance in Office.

21ST CENTURY MODERN LANGUAGE

It is prohibited for Senators and Representatives to have any other government job that was created while they were in office. They are also prohibited to get any job that pays higher wages when they were in office. It is prohibited for an officer in the U.S. Armed Forces to be a member of the House of Representatives or be a Senator at the same time as their military service.

 KINGDOM DECLARATION™

In the name of Jesus Christ, on behalf of the United States of America, I declare it is prohibited for Senators and Representatives to have any other government job while they are in office.

In the name of Jesus Christ, on behalf of the United States of America, I declare it is prohibited for Senators and Representatives to have any other government job that pays higher wages when they are in office.

In the name of Jesus Christ, on behalf of the United States of America, I declare it is prohibited for an officer in the U.S. Armed Forces to be a member of the House of Representatives or be a Senator at the same time as their military service.

§ Section 7: Revenue Bills

Clause 1

 1787 Transcription

All Bills for raising Revenue shall originate in the House of Representatives; but the Senate may propose or concur with Amendments as on other Bills.

 21st Century Modern Language

All Bills for generating revenue or collecting taxes shall originate in the House of Representatives. However, the Senate may propose amendments or agree with the Bill just as it can pertaining to other Bills.

 Kingdom Declaration™

In the name of Jesus Christ, on behalf of the United States of America, I declare all Bills for generating revenue or collecting taxes will originate in the House of Representatives.

In the name of Jesus Christ, on behalf of the United States of America, I declare the members of the House of Representatives are God-loving and God-fearing people.

In the name of Jesus Christ, on behalf of the United States of America, I declare the U.S. government will use tax payer's money wisely.

In the name of Jesus Christ, on behalf of the United States of America, I declare the U.S. government will stop funding satanic initiatives with tax payer's money.

In the name of Jesus Christ, on behalf of the United States of America, I declare the U.S. government will use tax payer's money to help people, make our nation greater, and advance God's Kingdom.

In the name of Jesus Christ, on behalf of the United States of America, I declare the Senate may propose amendments or agree with the Bill.

In the name of Jesus Christ, on behalf of the United States of America, I declare the members in the Senate will be anointed by God.

CLAUSE 2

 1787 TRANSCRIPTION

Every Bill which shall have passed the House of Representatives and the Senate, shall, before it become a Law, be presented to the President of the United States; If he approve he shall sign it, but if not he shall return it, with his Objections to that House in which it shall have originated, who shall enter the Objections at large on their Journal, and proceed to reconsider it. If after such Reconsideration two thirds of that House shall agree to pass the Bill, it shall be sent, together with the Objections, to the other House, by which it shall likewise be reconsidered, and if approved by two thirds of that House, it shall become a Law.

But in all such Cases the Votes of both Houses shall be determined by Yeas and Nays, and the Names of the Persons voting for and against the Bill shall be entered on the Journal of each House respectively. If any Bill shall not be returned by the President within ten Days (Sundays excepted) after it shall have been presented to him, the Same shall be a Law, in like Manner as if he had signed it, unless the Congress by their Adjournment prevent its Return, in which Case it shall not be a Law.

21ST CENTURY MODERN LANGUAGE

Every Bill that passes both the House of Representatives and the Senate shall go to the President of the United States. If the President approves and signs the Bill it will become law. If the President does not approve the Bill, his reasons for objecting the Bill shall be written down. The President will then need to send it back to the House or Senate depending on where the Bill originated. The House or Senate will then write the objections of the President in their journal. The law will then be discussed at an additional time.

During the discussion, if two thirds of a House votes for the Bill, then it shall go to the other House. All objections the President wrote will need to be included when it is presented to the other House. That House will re-examine the law and take another vote. If two thirds of that House votes to approve the Bill then it will take effect as law.

For these types of cases, each lawmaker's name and vote will be recorded in the journal. The record will State if the individual voted, "Yes" or "No" for the Bill.

The President will be allotted ten days to sign a Bill that comes from Congress. If the President does not sign or return a Bill to Congress in those ten days, then the Bill will become a law without his signing. Sunday is not counted in the ten day time period.

If Congress has returned home during the ten day period and the President is unable to return the Bill with the objections, then it shall not become law.

 Kingdom Declaration™

In the name of Jesus Christ, on behalf of the United States of America, I declare every Bill that passes both the House of Representatives and the Senate shall go to the President of the United States.

In the name of Jesus Christ, on behalf of the United States of America, I declare the President of the United States has Godly wisdom and discernment.

In the name of Jesus Christ, on behalf of the United States of America, I declare the Bills that pass both the House of Representatives and the Senate will be for the glory of the Heavenly Father, Jesus, and Holy Spirit.

In the name of Jesus Christ, on behalf of the United States of America, I declare the President will only approve and sign Bills that are Holy Spirit inspired.

In the name of Jesus Christ, on behalf of the United States of America, I declare the President will reject all Bills that have a satanic agenda.

In the name of Jesus Christ, on behalf of the United States of America, I declare the President will write down the reasons for objecting Bills.

In the name of Jesus Christ, on behalf of the United States of America, I declare Congress will not propose Bills that harm people.

In the name of Jesus Christ, on behalf of the United States of America, I declare evil Bills and laws will not need to be discussed an additional time.

In the name of Jesus Christ, on behalf of the United States of America, I declare evil Bills and laws in the works to cease now.

In the name of Jesus Christ, on behalf of the United States of America, I declare all Bills coming from Congress will be Holy Spirit inspired.

In the name of Jesus Christ, on behalf of the United States of America, I declare the President will not sign any Bill from Congress that is satanically inspired.

CLAUSE 3

 1787 TRANSCRIPTION

Every Order, Resolution, or Vote to which the Concurrence of the Senate and House of Representatives may be necessary (except on a question of Adjournment) shall be presented to the President of the United States; and before the Same shall take Effect, shall be approved by him, or being disapproved by him, shall be repassed by two thirds of the Senate and House of Representatives, according to the Rules and Limitations prescribed in the Case of a Bill.

21ST CENTURY MODERN LANGUAGE

All of the orders, resolutions, or votes that Congress make shall go to the U.S. President except on a question of adjourning.

The President must approve the orders, resolutions, or votes from Congress in order to go into effect. However, if the President does not approve, but two thirds of the Senate and the House of Representatives approve it, then it shall become a law.

 ## KINGDOM DECLARATION™

In the name of Jesus Christ, on behalf of the United States of America, I declare all orders, resolutions, or votes Congress makes shall go to the U.S. President except on a question of adjourning.

In the name of Jesus Christ, on behalf of the United States of America, I declare the orders, resolution, or votes from Congress will be Holy Spirit inspired.

In the name of Jesus Christ, on behalf of the United States of America, I declare the President must approve the orders, resolutions, or votes from Congress in order for them to go into effect.

In the name of Jesus Christ, on behalf of the United States of America, I declare wisdom for the President to determine which orders, resolutions, or votes should go into effect.

In the name of Jesus Christ, on behalf of the United States of America, I declare an outpouring of the Holy Spirit to invade the President, Senate, and House of Representatives.

§ SECTION 8: POWERS OF CONGRESS

CLAUSE 1

1787 TRANSCRIPTION

The Congress shall have Power To lay and collect Taxes, Duties, Imposts and Excises, to pay the Debts and provide for the common Defence and general Welfare of the United States; but all Duties, Imposts and Excises shall be uniform throughout the United States;

21ST CENTURY MODERN LANGUAGE

Congress has the power to determine what taxes to create and how to collect the taxes. For example, they can create taxes on items imported into the country. They can also create taxes on items made inside the United States. Congress can collect these taxes to pay debt acquired by the United States. They can also pay for military defense and general well being of the country. The taxes Congress creates shall be the same throughout the entire United States.

Kingdom Declaration™

In the name of Jesus Christ, on behalf of the United States of America, I declare a Holy Spirit outpouring in Congress.

In the name of Jesus Christ, on behalf of the United States of America, I declare Congress has the power to determine what taxes to create and how to collect them.

In the name of Jesus Christ, on behalf of the United States of America, I declare divine wisdom over each member of Congress.

In the name of Jesus Christ, on behalf of the United States of America, I declare Congress knows exactly what new taxes need to be created, if any.

In the name of Jesus Christ, on behalf of the United States of America, I declare Congress can collect these taxes to pay for debt acquired by the United States.

In the name of Jesus Christ, on behalf of the United States of America, I declare the United States will be debt free.

In the name of Jesus Christ, on behalf of the United States of America, I declare the government will steward finances judiciously, with constraint, and without fraud.

In the name of Jesus Christ, on behalf of the United States of America, I declare these taxes can be used to pay for military defense.

In the name of Jesus Christ, on behalf of the United States of America, I declare the Lord will place His hand of protection over the United States.

In the name of Jesus Christ, on behalf of the United States of America, I declare these taxes can be used for the general well being of the country.

In the name of Jesus Christ, on behalf of the United States of America, I declare any tax Congress creates will be the same for each State throughout the entire United States.

CLAUSE 2

1787 TRANSCRIPTION

To borrow Money on the credit of the United States;

21ST CENTURY MODERN LANGUAGE

Congress can borrow money on the credit of the United States.

Kingdom Declaration™

In the name of Jesus Christ, on behalf of the United States of America, I declare Congress can borrow money on the credit of the United States.

In the name of Jesus Christ, on behalf of the United States of America, I declare Congress will stay within a reasonable and responsible budget and will not borrow money on the credit of the United States.

Clause 3

 ### 1787 Transcription

To regulate Commerce with foreign Nations, and among the several States, and with the Indian Tribes;

 ### 21st Century Modern Language

Congress can make rules on how the United States trades with foreign nations. They can also make rules about trading among the various U.S. States as well as with Native American tribes.

Kingdom Declaration™

In the name of Jesus Christ, on behalf of the United States of America, I declare Congress can make rules on how the United States trades with foreign nations.

In the name of Jesus Christ, on behalf of the United States of America, I declare the rules made will benefit both the United States and the countries we are trading with.

In the name of Jesus Christ, on behalf of the United States of America, I declare Congress can make rules about trading among the various U.S. States as well as with Native American tribes.

In the name of Jesus Christ, on behalf of the United States of America, I declare all rules Congress have made that are of evil intent will dissolve.

Clause 4

 ### 1787 Transcription

To establish an uniform Rule of Naturalization, and uniform Laws on the subject of Bankruptcies throughout the United States;

21ST CENTURY MODERN LANGUAGE

Congress has the power to set up rules for foreign immigrants to become naturalized citizens. The rules and process will be the same in each State. Congress also has the power to set up laws regarding bankruptcies. The bankruptcy laws will be the same in each State.

KINGDOM DECLARATION™

In the name of Jesus Christ, on behalf of the United States of America, I declare Congress has the power to set up rules for foreign immigrants to become U.S. citizens.

In the name of Jesus Christ, on behalf of the United States of America, I declare all illegal immigrants who are here to harm the United States will be routed out.

In the name of Jesus Christ, on behalf of the United States of America, I declare all illegal immigrants living in the United States who will be a blessing to our nation will begin the process of naturalization.

In the name of Jesus Christ, on behalf of the United States of America, I declare the rules and process for naturalization is the same in each State.

In the name of Jesus Christ, on behalf of the United States of America, I declare Congress has the power to set up laws regarding bankruptcies.

In the name of Jesus Christ, on behalf of the United States of America, I declare the bankruptcy laws will be the same in each State.

In the name of Jesus Christ, on behalf of the United States of America, I declare the United States will not go bankrupt.

In the name of Jesus Christ, on behalf of the United States of America, I declare a revitalization of wealth for Godly purposes in each State of America.

CLAUSE 5

1787 TRANSCRIPTION

To coin Money, regulate the Value thereof, and of foreign Coin, and fix the Standard of Weights and Measures;

21st Century Modern Language

Congress has the power to coin money. Congress has the power to determine the value of U.S. coins compared to international coins. Congress has the power to establish a standard for weights and measures.

Kingdom Declaration™

In the name of Jesus Christ, on behalf of the United States of America, I declare Congress has the power to coin money.

In the name of Jesus Christ, on behalf of the United States of America, I declare Congress has the power to determine the value of U.S. coins compared to international coins.

In the name of Jesus Christ, on behalf of the United States of America, I declare Congress has the power to establish a standard for weights and measures.

In the name of Jesus Christ, on behalf of the United States of America, I declare Congress has established a perfect and just standard for weights and measures. (See Deuteronomy 25:15.)

Clause 6

1787 Transcription

To provide for the Punishment of counterfeiting the Securities and current Coin of the United States;

21st Century Modern Language

Congress has the power to decide the punishment for any person who might make counterfeit coins or paper currency of the United States of America.

Kingdom Declaration™

In the name of Jesus Christ, on behalf of the United States of America, I declare Congress has the power to decide the punishment for any person who tries to make counterfeit coins of paper currency of the United States of America.

In the name of Jesus Christ, on behalf of the United States of America, I declare people will not desire to create counterfeit currencies.

In the name of Jesus Christ, on behalf of the United States of America, I declare financial blessings over the United States.

CLAUSE 7

1787 Transcription

To establish Post Offices and post Roads;

21st Century Modern Language

Congress has the power to create post offices and postal roads.

Kingdom Declaration™

In the name of Jesus Christ, on behalf of the United States of America, I declare Congress has the power to create post offices and postal roads.

In the name of Jesus Christ, on behalf of the United States of America, I declare the U.S. Post Office will not be used for cheating or corruption during election times.

In the name of Jesus Christ, on behalf of the United States of America, I declare the Lord will do a mighty work to eliminate the corruption from the U.S. Post Office.

Clause 8

1787 Transcription

To promote the Progress of Science and useful Arts, by securing for limited Times to Authors and Inventors the exclusive Right to their respective Writings and Discoveries;

21st Century Modern Language

Congress shall promote the progress of science and arts. They will grant copyrights to authors and patents to inventors. The granting of copyrights and patents will give the authors and inventors rights to their writings and inventions. These rights will be for a limited time period. These rights will also prevent other people from using their writings or inventions without proper compensation.

KINGDOM DECLARATION™

In the name of Jesus Christ, on behalf of the United States of America, I declare Congress shall promote the progress of science and arts.

In the name of Jesus Christ, on behalf of the United States of America, I declare Congress will grant copyrights and patents to the rightful owners.

In the name of Jesus Christ, on behalf of the United States of America, I declare the copyrights and patents will protect the owners from other people infringing on their rights.

In the name of Jesus Christ, on behalf of the United States of America, I declare people who need to write wholesome works will begin the process.

In the name of Jesus Christ, on behalf of the United States of America, I declare people who need to invent items for the benefit of humanity will begin the process.

Clause 9

1787 Transcription

To constitute Tribunals inferior to the supreme Court;

21st Century Modern Language

Congress has the power to establish courts lower in caliber than the Supreme Court.

Kingdom Declaration™

In the name of Jesus Christ, on behalf of the United States of America, I declare Congress has the power to establish courts lower than the Supreme Court.

In the name of Jesus Christ, on behalf of the United States of America, I declare a holiness movement to sweep through the court system and justice department.

In the name of Jesus Christ, on behalf of the United States of America, I declare corruption in the courts will be exposed.

In the name of Jesus Christ, on behalf of the United States of America, I declare the people who do not execute true justice will be exposed and prosecuted.

In the name of Jesus Christ, on behalf of the United States of America, I declare those operating in the court systems will not be defiled by taking bribes. (See Deuteronomy 16:19.)

CLAUSE 10

1787 TRANSCRIPTION

To define and punish Piracies and Felonies committed on the high Seas, and Offences against the Law of Nations;

21ST CENTURY MODERN LANGUAGE

Congress has the power to establish laws pertaining to piracy and felonies while at sea. Congress will also have the power to punish people who disregard or break international laws.

KINGDOM DECLARATION™

In the name of Jesus Christ, on behalf of the United States of America, I declare Congress has the power to establish laws pertaining to piracy and felonies while at sea.

In the name of Jesus Christ, on behalf of the United States of America, I declare Congress has the power to punish people who disregard or break international laws.

CLAUSE 11

1787 TRANSCRIPTION

To declare War, grant Letters of Marque and Reprisal, and make Rules concerning Captures on Land and Water;

21ST CENTURY MODERN LANGUAGE

Congress has the power to declare war. Congress also has the power to grant Letters of Marque. (A Letter of Marque is a license granted to a private person to fit out an armed ship to plunder the enemy.) Congress has the power to establish laws and rules regarding the capture of either people or property. These laws and rules are effective both on land and sea and are fair and just.

Kingdom Declaration™

In the name of Jesus Christ, on behalf of the United States of America, I declare Congress has the power to declare war.

In the name of Jesus Christ, on behalf of the United States of America, I declare Congress has the power to grant Letters of Marque.

In the name of Jesus Christ, on behalf of the United States of America, I declare Congress has the power to establish laws and rules regarding the capture of either people or property.

In the name of Jesus Christ, on behalf of the United States of America, I declare the laws and rules are effective both on land and sea.

Clause 12

1787 Transcription

To raise and support Armies, but no Appropriation of Money to that Use shall be for a longer Term than two Years;

21st Century Modern Language

Congress has the power to raise funds and pay for an army. However, Congress does not have the power to vote for finances for armies in a time span greater than two years.

Kingdom Declaration™

In the name of Jesus Christ, on behalf of the United States of America, I declare Congress has the power to raise funds and pay for an army.

In the name of Jesus Christ, on behalf of the United States of America, I declare Congress does not have the power to vote for finances for armies in a time span greater than two years.

In the name of Jesus Christ, on behalf of the United States of America, I declare the U.S. Army will have more than enough resources and finances needed to protect the citizens, properties, and resources of the USA.

CLAUSE 13

1787 TRANSCRIPTION
To provide and maintain a Navy;

21ST CENTURY MODERN LANGUAGE
Congress has the power to develop and fund a navy.

KINGDOM DECLARATION™
In the name of Jesus Christ, on behalf of the United States of America, I declare Congress has the power to develop and fund a navy.

In the name of Jesus Christ, on behalf of the United States of America, I declare the U.S. Navy will have more than enough resources and finances needed to protect the citizens, properties, and resources of the USA.

In the name of Jesus Christ, on behalf of the United States of America, I declare an outpouring of the Holy Spirit to sweep through every branch of the United States Armed Forces.

Clause 14

1787 Transcription

To make Rules for the Government and Regulation of the land and naval Forces;

21st Century Modern Language

Congress has the power to establish laws and rules for the government and regulations of land and naval forces.

Kingdom Declaration™

In the name of Jesus Christ, on behalf of the United States of America, I declare Congress has the power to establish laws and rules for the government and regulations of land and naval forces.

Clause 15

1787 Transcription

To provide for calling forth the Militia to execute the Laws of the Union, suppress Insurrections and repel Invasions;

21st Century Modern Language

Congress has the power to activate the National Guard and State army to enforce laws, combat insurrection, and war against foreign armies invading the United States of America.

Kingdom Declaration™

In the name of Jesus Christ, on behalf of the United States of America, I declare Congress has the power to activate the National Guard and State army to enforce laws, combat insurrection, and war against foreign armies invading the United States of America.

In the name of Jesus Christ, on behalf of the United States of America, I declare peace over the United States.

In the name of Jesus Christ, on behalf of the United States of America, I declare all evil people in the U.S. government attacking the citizens of the USA to be exposed now.

In the name of Jesus Christ, on behalf of the United States of America, I declare Congress will not use their power for corruption or a means of controlling people.

In the name of Jesus Christ, on behalf of the United States of America, I declare the United States will not be invaded by hostile armies.

In the name of Jesus Christ, on behalf of the United States of America, I declare all evil people and groups plotting to destroy America will be caught and prosecuted.

In the name of Jesus Christ, on behalf of the United States of America, I declare the light of Jesus will shine in the dark areas.

CLAUSE 16

1787 TRANSCRIPTION

To provide for organizing, arming, and disciplining, the Militia, and for governing such Part of them as may be employed in the Service of the United States, reserving to the States respectively, the Appointment of the Officers, and the Authority of training the Militia according to the discipline prescribed by Congress;

21st Century Modern Language

Congress has the power to organize, to provide weapons, and discipline the militia. (In the context of the U.S. Constitution a militia is defined as a body of citizens organized for military service.) Congress also has the power to oversee or govern the militia that is in service to the U.S. government. Congress will permit each State to appoint their own officers over the State run militias. Each State will then train their own militia with Congress acting as an overseer.

Kingdom Declaration™

In the name of Jesus Christ, on behalf of the United States of America, I declare Congress has the power to organize, to provide weapons, and discipline militias.

In the name of Jesus Christ, on behalf of the United States of America, I declare all evil militias plotting destruction against the United States or citizens to be exposed and stopped, now.

In the name of Jesus Christ, on behalf of the United States of America, I declare groups of spiritual warriors who love America will arise.

In the name of Jesus Christ, on behalf of the United States of America, I declare all enemies against America will be taken down by the hand of God.

In the name of Jesus Christ, on behalf of the United States of America, I declare Congress has the power to oversee or govern the militia that is in service to the U.S. government.

In the name of Jesus Christ, on behalf of the United States of America, I declare Congress will permit each State to appoint their own officers over the State run militias.

In the name of Jesus Christ, on behalf of the United States of America, I declare each State will train their own militia while Congress acts as an overseer.

CLAUSE 17

1787 TRANSCRIPTION

To exercise exclusive Legislation in all Cases whatsoever, over such District (not exceeding ten Miles square) as may, by Cession of particular States, and the Acceptance of Congress, become the Seat of the Government of the United States, and to exercise like Authority over all Places purchased by the Consent of the Legislature of the State in which the Same shall be, for the Erection of Forts, Magazines, Arsenals, dock-Yards, and other needful Buildings;—And

21ST CENTURY MODERN LANGUAGE

Congress has the power to make legislation for the Capital of the United States of America. The district will be created from property given by the States. The area shall not exceed ten square miles. The district will become the Capital and the location where the U.S. government conducts business. Congress will have sovereignty over it. They will be able to construct forts, store weapons and ammunition, build docks, and make other needful buildings.

👑 KINGDOM DECLARATION™

In the name of Jesus Christ, on behalf of the United States of America, I declare Congress has the power to make laws for the Capital of the United States of America.

In the name of Jesus Christ, on behalf of the United States of America, I declare all business occurring inside the U.S. Capital inspired by satan will be exposed and defeated.

In the name of Jesus Christ, on behalf of the United States of America, I declare business that occurs in the U.S. Capital will be Holy Spirit inspired.

In the name of Jesus Christ, on behalf of the United States of America, I declare that Congress might have sovereignty over the Capital, but the Heavenly Father, Jesus, and Holy Spirit are sovereign to all things.

CLAUSE 18

1787 TRANSCRIPTION

To make all Laws which shall be necessary and proper for carrying into Execution the foregoing Powers, and all other Powers vested by this Constitution in the Government of the United States, or in any Department or Officer thereof.

21st Century Modern Language

Congress has the power to establish the laws that are necessary to carry out the powers aforementioned. Congress also has the power to establish the laws that are necessary to carry out the additional powers this Constitution gives the government.

 ## Kingdom Declaration™

In the name of Jesus Christ, on behalf of the United States of America, I declare Congress has the power to establish the laws that are necessary to carry out the powers aforementioned.

In the name of Jesus Christ, on behalf of the United States of America, I declare Congress also has the power to establish the laws that are necessary to carry out the additional powers this Constitution gives the government.

§ SECTION 9: LIMITS ON CONGRESS

CLAUSE 1

1787 TRANSCRIPTION

The Migration or Importation of such Persons as any of the States now existing shall think proper to admit, shall not be prohibited by the Congress prior to the Year one thousand eight hundred and eight, but a Tax or duty may be imposed on such Importation, not exceeding ten dollars for each Person.

21ST CENTURY MODERN LANGUAGE

Congress does not have the power to stop the various States from importing slaves before the year 1808. Congress can put a tax on bringing in such people. For people brought in, the tax may not exceed $10 per person.

(Note: This clause relates to the slave trade. It prevented Congress from restricting the importation of enslaved people before 1808. However, in 1807 the international slave trade was blocked.

Ultimately, the enslavement of African people ended in 1865 when the 13th Amendment took effect. Please see Book 3 in the *Kingdom Declaration Series™* entitled, *Declaring Amendments 11-27*.)

 KINGDOM DECLARATION™

In the name of Jesus Christ, on behalf of the United States of America, we repent for importing people into our nation to work as slaves.

In the name of Jesus Christ, on behalf of the United States of America, we repent for enslaving men, women, boys, and girls in the sex trade.

In the name of Jesus Christ, on behalf of the United States of America, we repent for enslaving people through human trafficking.

In the name of Jesus Christ, on behalf of the United States of America, we repent for going into financial debt and becoming slaves to other people and big corporations.

In the name of Jesus Christ, on behalf of the United States of America, we choose to forgive all people or businesses that enslaved us in any way.

In the name of Jesus Christ, on behalf of the United States of America, we choose to forgive any person or business who acted as a taskmaster over us.

In the name of Jesus Christ, on behalf of the United States of America, I declare the government will not enslave the people of this nation.

CLAUSE 2

 1787 TRANSCRIPTION

The Privilege of the Writ of Habeas Corpus shall not be suspended, unless when in Cases of Rebellion or Invasion the public Safety may require it.

 21ST CENTURY MODERN LANGUAGE

People may not be kept in jail without a hearing by a judge. This is the privilege of Writ of Habeas Corpus which means there is legal protection for detained people to argue in court that they are being held illegally. However, this protection is void if there is a rebellion, uprising, or enemy invasion.

KINGDOM DECLARATION™

In the name of Jesus Christ, on behalf of the United States of America, I declare people may not be kept in jail without a hearing by a judge.

In the name of Jesus Christ, on behalf of the United States of America, I declare there is legal protection for detained people to argue in court that they are being held illegally.

CLAUSE 3

1787 TRANSCRIPTION

No Bill of Attainder or ex post facto Law shall be passed.

21st CENTURY MODERN LANGUAGE

There shall not be any laws that convict a person of a guilty crime without a proper trial.

There shall not be any laws that makes something illegal after it has already been done, when it was not initially illegal.

Kingdom Declaration™

In the name of Jesus Christ, on behalf of the United States of America, I declare there shall not be any laws that convict a person of a guilty crime without a proper trial.

In the name of Jesus Christ, on behalf of the United States of America, I declare there shall not be any laws that makes something illegal after it has already been done, when it was not initially illegal.

Clause 4

1787 Transcription

No Capitation, or other direct, Tax shall be laid, unless in Proportion to the Census or Enumeration herein before directed to be taken. (Note: This was changed by the 16th Amendment.)

21st Century Modern Language

There shall not be any personal or other direct tax unless it is proportionate to the total number of individuals in a State determined by an official census. (Note: This was changed by the 16th Amendment.)

Kingdom Declaration™

Clause 4 was modified by Amendment 16. Please see Book 3 in the *Kingdom Declaration Series*™ entitled, *Declaring Amendments 11-27*.

Clause 5

1787 Transcription

No Tax or Duty shall be laid on articles exported from any State.

21st Century Modern Language

There shall not be any taxes on items exported from any State.

Kingdom Declaration™

In the name of Jesus Christ, on behalf of the United States of America, I declare there shall not be any taxes on items exported from any State.

CLAUSE 6

1787 Transcription

No Preference shall be given by any Regulation of Commerce or Revenue to the Ports of one State over those of another: nor shall Vessels bound to, or from, one State, be obliged to enter, clear, or pay Duties in another.

21st Century Modern Language

There shall not be any favoritism shown to one State over another State in regards to their ports. The ports of all of the individual States shall be treated equally in regulations or taxes. Ships entering or leaving one State shall not have to enter another State's port, nor shall they have to pay taxes to enter the port of another State.

Kingdom Declaration™

In the name of Jesus Christ, on behalf of the United States of America, I declare there shall not be any favoritism shown to one State over another State in regards to their ports.

In the name of Jesus Christ, on behalf of the United States of America, I declare the ports of all of the individual States shall be treated equally in regulations or taxes.

In the name of Jesus Christ, on behalf of the United States of America, I declare ships entering or leaving one State shall not have to enter another State's port, nor shall they have to pay taxes to enter the port of another State.

CLAUSE 7

1787 TRANSCRIPTION

No Money shall be drawn from the Treasury, but in Consequence of Appropriations made by Law; and a regular Statement and Account of the Receipts and Expenditures of all public Money shall be published from time to time.

21ST CENTURY MODERN LANGUAGE

Money in the United States Treasury cannot be withdrawn or spent unless a law is passed by Congress to do so. Congress is required to publish a Statement and account of the handling of all public finances.

Kingdom Declaration™

In the name of Jesus Christ, on behalf of the United States of America, I declare money in the United States Treasury cannot be withdrawn or spent unless a law is passed by Congress to do so.

In the name of Jesus Christ, on behalf of the United States of America, I declare Congress is required to publish a Statement and account of the handling of all public finances.

Clause 8

 1787 Transcription

No Title of Nobility shall be granted by the United States: And no Person holding any Office of Profit or Trust under them, shall, without the Consent of the Congress, accept of any present, Emolument, Office, or Title, of any kind whatever, from any King, Prince, or foreign State.

21st Century Modern Language

The United States of America shall not give anyone a title of nobility or royalty.

No person serving in any office of the U.S. government is permitted to accept a gift, pay, job, or title of any kind from any foreign country or leader.

Kingdom Declaration™

In the name of Jesus Christ, on behalf of the United States of America, I declare the U.S. shall not give anyone a title of nobility or royalty.

In the name of Jesus Christ, on behalf of the United States of America, I declare no person serving in any office of the U.S. government is permitted to accept a gift, pay, job, or title of any kind from any foreign country or leader.

In the name of Jesus Christ, on behalf of the United States of America, I declare that people in U.S. governmental positions will not accept bribes.

In the name of Jesus Christ, on behalf of the United States of America, I declare that people in U.S. governmental positions who have accepted bribes and illegally profited while in office will be exposed and prosecuted.

§ SECTION 10: POWERS PROHIBITED

CLAUSE 1

1787 TRANSCRIPTION

No State shall enter into any Treaty, Alliance, or Confederation; grant Letters of Marque and Reprisal; coin Money; emit Bills of Credit; make any Thing but gold and silver Coin a Tender in Payment of Debts; pass any Bill of Attainder, ex post facto Law, or Law impairing the Obligation of Contracts, or grant any Title of Nobility.

21ST CENTURY MODERN LANGUAGE

U.S. States cannot make treaties or alliances with foreign nations.

U.S. States cannot grant permission to a foreign country's military forces to cross their borders.

U.S. States cannot coin or print paper money.

U.S. States cannot ask for anything except gold and silver coins for the payment of debts.

U.S. States cannot pass any laws that convict a person of a crime without a proper trial.

U.S. States cannot create laws that make certain actions illegal after the actions were already done.

U.S. States cannot make any laws that limit the obligations found in a contract.

U.S. States cannot give any person a title of nobility or royalty.

Kingdom Declaration™

In the name of Jesus Christ, on behalf of the United States of America, I declare U.S. States cannot make treaties or alliances with foreign nations.

In the name of Jesus Christ, on behalf of the United States of America, I declare U.S. States cannot grant permission to a foreign country's military forces to cross their borders.

In the name of Jesus Christ, on behalf of the United States of America, I declare U.S. States cannot coin or print paper money.

In the name of Jesus Christ, on behalf of the United States of America, I declare U.S. States cannot ask for anything except gold and silver coins for the payment of debts.

In the name of Jesus Christ, on behalf of the United States of America, I declare U.S. States cannot pass any laws that convict a person of a crime without a proper trial.

In the name of Jesus Christ, on behalf of the United States of America, I declare U.S. States cannot create laws that make certain actions illegal after the actions were already done.

In the name of Jesus Christ, on behalf of the United States of America, I declare U.S. States cannot make any laws that limit the obligations found in a contract.

In the name of Jesus Christ, on behalf of the United States of America, I declare U.S. States cannot give any person a title of nobility or royalty.

Article 1 -127-

CLAUSE 2

 1787 TRANSCRIPTION

No State shall, without the Consent of the Congress, lay any Imposts or Duties on Imports or Exports, except what may be absolutely necessary for executing it's inspection Laws: and the net Produce of all Duties and Imposts, laid by any State on Imports or Exports, shall be for the Use of the Treasury of the United States; and all such Laws shall be subject to the Revision and Controul of the Congress.

 21ST CENTURY MODERN LANGUAGE

Unless Congress agrees, U.S. States cannot pass or collect taxes on imports or exports, except the essential taxes necessary for inspection laws.

After paying for their own expenses, the tax money obtained from any of these duties made by the States are for the U.S. national treasury.

All the laws that U.S. States make that are similar to these can be modified or controlled by Congress.

KINGDOM DECLARATION™

In the name of Jesus Christ, on behalf of the United States of America, I declare unless Congress agrees, U.S. States cannot pass or collect taxes on imports or exports, except the essential taxes necessary for inspection laws.

In the name of Jesus Christ, on behalf of the United States of America, I declare after paying for their own expenses, the tax money obtained from any of these duties made by the States are for the U.S. national treasury.

In the name of Jesus Christ, on behalf of the United States of America, I declare all the laws that U.S. States make that are similar to these can be modified or controlled by Congress and shall be just and honest.

CLAUSE 3

 1787 TRANSCRIPTION

No State shall, without the Consent of Congress, lay any Duty of Tonnage, keep Troops, or Ships of War in time of Peace, enter into any Agreement or Compact with another State, or with a foreign Power, or engage in War, unless actually invaded, or in such imminent Danger as will not admit of delay.

 21ST CENTURY MODERN LANGUAGE

Unless Congress agrees, U.S. States cannot tax ships.

U.S. States cannot keep soldiers or ships of war during a time of peace.

U.S. States cannot enter into any agreement with another State or foreign country.

U.S. States cannot go to war unless the State is invaded and there is not enough time to get Congress' approval due to the immediate danger.

KINGDOM DECLARATION™

In the name of Jesus Christ, on behalf of the United States of America, I declare U.S. States cannot tax ships.

In the name of Jesus Christ, on behalf of the United States of America, I declare U.S. States cannot keep soldiers or ships of war during a time of peace.

In the name of Jesus Christ, on behalf of the United States of America, I declare U.S. States cannot enter into any agreement with another State or foreign country.

In the name of Jesus Christ, on behalf of the United States of America, I declare U.S. States cannot go to war unless the State is invaded and there is not enough time to get Congress' approval due to the immediate danger.

Article 2
The Executive Branch

§ Section 1: The President

Clause 1

1787 Transcription

The executive Power shall be vested in a President of the United States of America. He shall hold his Office during the Term of four Years, and, together with the Vice President, chosen for the same Term, be elected, as follows:

21st Century Modern Language

The United States of America shall have an executive branch of government. The power for this branch is to be held by the President of the United States. The President's term of office shall be four years. Likewise, the term for a Vice President will also be four years. This is how the election will occur:

KINGDOM DECLARATION™

In the name of Jesus Christ, on behalf of the United States of America, I declare that we will have an executive branch of government.

In the name of Jesus Christ, on behalf of the United States of America, I declare the power for this branch is to be held by the President of the United States.

In the name of Jesus Christ, on behalf of the United States of America, I declare the President will lead our nation in righteousness as outlined according to the Holy Bible.

In the name of Jesus Christ, on behalf of the United States of America, I declare the President's term of office shall be four years.

In the name of Jesus Christ, on behalf of the United States of America, I declare the term for a Vice President will also be four years.

CLAUSE 2

1787 TRANSCRIPTION

Each State shall appoint, in such Manner as the Legislature thereof may direct, a Number of Electors, equal to the whole Number of Senators and Representatives to which the State may be entitled in the Congress: but no Senator or Representative, or Person holding an Office of Trust or Profit under the United States, shall be appointed an Elector.

21ST CENTURY MODERN LANGUAGE

Each U.S. State will have a certain number of Electors in which they can choose the President. Each individual State will have the power on how to choose the Electors. The total number of Electors is equal to the number of Senators and Representatives the State has in Congress. Senators and Representatives are prohibited from being Electors. Individuals who hold an office of trust or profit with the U.S. government are also disqualified from being an Elector.

Kingdom Declaration™

In the name of Jesus Christ, on behalf of the United States of America, I declare each U.S. State will have a certain number of Electors in which they can choose the President.

In the name of Jesus Christ, on behalf of the United States of America, I declare each individual State will have the power on how to choose the Electors.

In the name of Jesus Christ, on behalf of the United States of America, I declare the total number of Electors is equal to the number of Senators and Representatives the State has in Congress.

In the name of Jesus Christ, on behalf of the United States of America, I declare Senators and Representatives are prohibited from being Electors.

In the name of Jesus Christ, on behalf of the United States of America, I declare individuals who hold an office of trust or profit with the U.S. government are disqualified from being an Elector.

Clause 3

 1787 Transcription

The Electors shall meet in their respective States, and vote by Ballot for two Persons, of whom one at least shall not be an Inhabitant of the same State with themselves. And they shall make a List of all the Persons voted for, and of the Number of Votes for each; which List they shall sign and certify, and transmit sealed to the Seat of the Government of the United States, directed to the President of the Senate.

The President of the Senate shall, in the Presence of the Senate and House of Representatives, open all the Certificates, and the Votes shall then be counted. The Person having the greatest Number of Votes shall be the President, if such Number be a Majority of the whole Number of Electors appointed; and if there be more than one who have such Majority, and have an equal Number of Votes, then the House of Representatives shall immediately chuse by Ballot one of them for President; and if no Person have a Majority, then from the five highest on the List the said House shall in like Manner chuse the President. But in chusing the President, the Votes shall be taken by States, the Representation from each State having one Vote; A quorum for this Purpose shall consist of a Member or Members from two thirds of the States, and a Majority of all the States shall be necessary to a Choice.

In every Case, after the Choice of the President, the Person having the greatest Number of Votes of the Electors shall be the Vice President. But if there should remain two or more who have equal Votes, the Senate shall chuse from them by Ballot the Vice President. (Note: Clause 3 was changed by the 12th Amendment.)

 21st Century Modern Language

In each U.S. State, the State's Electors shall gather together. The Electors shall vote for two people using written ballots. The two people must be from different States. The Electors are required to make a list of all the people they voted for. The Electors are to write down the number of votes each person got. The Electors are then required to sign the list, certify it, seal it, and send it to the Congress of the United Sates. The envelope is to be directed to the President of the Senate. The President of the Senate is required to open the envelope with the certified votes in the sight of all the

Senators and Representatives of Congress. The votes are then to be counted. The person who received the highest number of votes shall become the President, if he has a majority of the votes.

If there is a tie and another person also has a majority of votes, then the House of Representatives is required by written ballot to choose one of the candidates to become President. If nobody has a majority of votes, then the House of Representatives will make the decision who will become President from the five people on the list who received the highest number of votes.

Choosing a President in this manner, each State shall have one vote. It is required that at least two thirds of all the States must have members present in order to vote. A majority of all the States must be in attendance to chose the President. After the President is chosen, the person with the second highest number of votes of the Electors shall become the Vice President. If there are two or more people with the same number of votes, then the Senate will be required to appoint the Vice President. (Note: Clause 3 was changed by the 12th Amendment.)

KINGDOM DECLARATION™

Clause 3 was modified by the 12th Amendment. Please see Book 3 in the *Kingdom Declaration Series™* entitled, *Declaring Amendments 11-27*.

 CLAUSE 4

 ### 1787 TRANSCRIPTION

The Congress may determine the Time of chusing the Electors, and the Day on which they shall give their Votes; which Day shall be the same throughout the United States.

 ### 21ST CENTURY MODERN LANGUAGE

Congress can determine the date the States choose their Electors. Congress can also determine the day when the Electors send in their votes.

The day Congress chooses for the Electors to send in their votes will be the same day throughout the entire United States.

Kingdom Declaration™

In the name of Jesus Christ, on behalf of the United States of America, I declare Congress determines the date the States choose their Electors.

In the name of Jesus Christ, on behalf of the United States of America, I declare Congress determines the day when the Electors send in their votes.

In the name of Jesus Christ, on behalf of the United States of America, I declare the day Congress chooses for the Electors to send in their votes will be the same day throughout the entire United States.

Clause 5

1787 Transcription

No Person except a natural born Citizen, or a Citizen of the United States, at the time of the Adoption of this Constitution, shall be eligible to the Office of President; neither shall any Person be eligible to that Office who shall not have attained to the Age of thirty five Years, and been fourteen Years a Resident within the United States.

21st Century Modern Language

Only an individual who is born in the United States of America, or is a citizen of the United States at the time of this Constitution, can become the U.S. President. All U.S. Presidents must be a minimum of thirty-five years of age or older. The U.S. President must have lived inside the United States for at least fourteen years.

Kingdom Declaration™

In the name of Jesus Christ, on behalf of the United States of America, I declare only an individual who is born in the United States of America can become the U.S. President.

In the name of Jesus Christ, on behalf of the United States of America, I declare all U.S. Presidents must be a minimum of thirty-five years of age or older.

In the name of Jesus Christ, on behalf of the United States of America, I declare the U.S. President must have lived inside the United States for at least fourteen years.

CLAUSE 6

1787 TRANSCRIPTION

In Case of the Removal of the President from Office, or of his Death, Resignation, or Inability to discharge the Powers and Duties of the said Office, the Same shall devolve on the Vice President, and the Congress may by Law provide for the Case of Removal, Death, Resignation or Inability, both of the President and Vice President, declaring what Officer shall then act as President, and such Officer shall act accordingly, until the Disability be removed, or a President shall be elected.

21ST CENTURY MODERN LANGUAGE

The Vice President of the United States shall do the same job and have the same authority as the U.S. President if the President is removed from office, dies, resigns, or is unable to do the job.

In the situation that both the U.S. President and Vice President are removed from office, die, resign, or are unable to do the job, Congress can make a law stating who shall do the President's job and have his authority. The person chosen by Congress shall act as

President until the U.S. President is able to perform the job, the U.S. Vice President is able to act as President, or a new U.S. President is elected.

Kingdom Declaration™

In the name of Jesus Christ, on behalf of the United States of America, I declare the U.S. Vice President shall do the same job and have the same authority as the U.S. President if the President is removed from office, dies, resigns, or is unable to do the job.

In the name of Jesus Christ, on behalf of the United States of America, I declare if both the U.S. President and Vice President are removed from office, die, resign, or are unable to do the job, Congress can make a law stating who shall do the President's job and have his authority.

In the name of Jesus Christ, on behalf of the United States of America, I declare the person chosen by Congress shall act as President until the U.S. President is able to perform the job, the U.S. Vice President is able to act as President, or a new U.S. President is elected.

In the name of Jesus Christ, on behalf of the United States of America, I declare our U.S. Presidents, Vice Presidents, and elected officials will have a heart for Jesus and lead the nation to the Heavenly Father.

CLAUSE 7

1787 TRANSCRIPTION

The President shall, at Stated Times, receive for his Services, a Compensation, which shall neither be encreased nor diminished during the Period for which he shall have been elected, and he shall not receive within that Period any other Emolument from the United States, or any of them.

21ST CENTURY MODERN LANGUAGE

The U.S. President shall receive wages for his services. The payment cannot be increased nor decreased during his term as President. While in office as President, he cannot receive any other salary or financial compensation from the United States as a whole, or individual States.

Kingdom Declaration™

In the name of Jesus Christ, on behalf of the United States of America, I declare the U.S. President shall receive wages for his services.

In the name of Jesus Christ, on behalf of the United States of America, I declare the President's payment cannot be increased nor decreased during his term as President.

In the name of Jesus Christ, on behalf of the United States of America, I declare while in office as President, he cannot receive any other salary or financial compensation from the United States as a whole, or individual States.

Clause 8

1787 Transcription

Before he enter on the Execution of his Office, he shall take the following Oath or Affirmation:—"I do solemnly swear (or affirm) that I will faithfully execute the Office of President of the United States, and will to the best of my Ability, preserve, protect and defend the Constitution of the United States."

21st Century Modern Language

Before the President takes his office, he must declare the following oath or affirmation:

"I do solemnly swear that I will faithfully execute the Office of President of the United States. I will to the best of my ability, preserve, protect, and defend the Constitution of the United States."

Kingdom Declaration™

In the name of Jesus Christ, on behalf of the United States of America, I declare the President will declare the following oath with sincerity of heart.

In the name of Jesus Christ, on behalf of the United States of America, I declare when the President speaks forth these words: "I do solemnly swear that I will faithfully execute the Office of President of the United States," his or her heart's desire will be to fulfill the oath he or she has made.

In the name of Jesus Christ, on behalf of the United States of America, I declare when the President speaks forth these words: "I will to the best of my ability, preserve, protect, and defend the Constitution of the United States," his or her heart's desire will be to fulfill the oath he or she has made.

In the name of Jesus Christ, on behalf of the United States of America, I declare people who do not have the desire to fulfill this Presidential vow will not become President of the United States.

In the name of Jesus Christ, on behalf of the United States of America, I declare people who do not have the best interests for America and her citizens will not become President of the United States.

§ SECTION 2: CIVILIAN POWER

CLAUSE 1

1787 TRANSCRIPTION

The President shall be Commander in Chief of the Army and Navy of the United States, and of the Militia of the several States, when called into the actual Service of the United States; he may require the Opinion, in writing, of the principal Officer in each of the executive Departments, upon any Subject relating to the Duties of their respective Offices, and he shall have Power to grant Reprieves and Pardons for Offences against the United States, except in Cases of Impeachment.

21ST CENTURY MODERN LANGUAGE

The President shall be the Commander in Chief of the United States' Army and Navy. The President shall also be in charge of the armies of each State when they are called upon to serve the United States. The U.S. President can also ask for written opinions of the leading officers in the executive departments on any topic that relates to their duties.

The President has the power to cancel or postpone a person condemned to death. The President has the power to pardon people who have been guilty of crimes held against the United States of America. However, this does not hold true in the case of an impeachment.

 KINGDOM DECLARATION™

In the name of Jesus Christ, on behalf of the United States of America, I declare the President shall be the Commander in Chief of the United States' Army and Navy.

In the name of Jesus Christ, on behalf of the United States of America, I declare the President shall be in charge of the armies of each State when they are called upon to serve the United States.

In the name of Jesus Christ, on behalf of the United States of America, I declare the President can ask for written opinions of the leading officers in the executive departments on any topic that relates to their duties.

In the name of Jesus Christ, on behalf of the United States of America, I declare the President has the power to cancel or postpone a person condemned to death.

In the name of Jesus Christ, on behalf of the United States of America, I declare the President has the power to pardon people who have been guilty of crimes held against the United States of America and will use Godly wisdom in any such cases.

Clause 2

1787 Transcription

He shall have Power, by and with the Advice and Consent of the Senate, to make Treaties, provided two thirds of the Senators present concur; and he shall nominate, and by and with the Advice and Consent of the Senate, shall appoint Ambassadors, other public Ministers and Consuls, Judges of the supreme Court, and all other Officers of the United States, whose Appointments are not herein otherwise provided for, and which shall be established by Law: but the Congress may by Law vest the Appointment of such inferior Officers, as they think proper, in the President alone, in the Courts of Law, or in the Heads of Departments.

21st Century Modern Language

The U.S. President has the power to make treaties with foreign nations. However, before a treaty can become a part of the law, two thirds of the Senators must approve the treaty.

With the advice and consent of the Senate, the U.S. President shall nominate and appoint ambassadors, public ministers, consuls, Judges of the Supreme Court, and all other officers of the United States. However, the exceptions are for those offices that the U.S. Constitution lists other methods of selecting. The U.S. President must hear advice from the Senate and have the Senate's consent to assign these job positions.

Congress can make a law to permit the U.S. President to appoint less important officers in the courts or the heads of departments without needing Senate approval.

👑 KINGDOM DECLARATION™

In the name of Jesus Christ, on behalf of the United States of America, I declare the U.S. President has the power to make treaties with foreign nations.

In the name of Jesus Christ, on behalf of the United States of America, I declare before a treaty can become a part of the law, two thirds of the Senators must approve the treaty.

In the name of Jesus Christ, on behalf of the United States of America, I declare with the advice and consent of the Senate, the U.S. President shall nominate and appoint ambassadors, public ministers, consuls, Judges of the Supreme Court, and all other officers of the United States.

In the name of Jesus Christ, on behalf of the United States of America, I declare the exceptions are for those offices that the U.S. Constitution lists other methods of selecting.

In the name of Jesus Christ, on behalf of the United States of America, I declare the U.S. President must hear advice from the Senate and have the Senate's consent to assign these job positions.

In the name of Jesus Christ, on behalf of the United States of America, I declare Congress can make a law to permit the U.S. President to appoint less important officers in the courts or the heads of departments without needing Senate approval.

CLAUSE 3

1787 TRANSCRIPTION

The President shall have Power to fill up all Vacancies that may happen during the Recess of the Senate, by granting Commissions which shall expire at the End of their next Session.

21ST CENTURY MODERN LANGUAGE

The U.S. President has the power to appoint people to offices that become vacant during the time period that the Senate is not in session. However, the President shall only appoint them for a short time as their terms shall expire at the end of the next session of the Senate.

KINGDOM DECLARATION™

In the name of Jesus Christ, on behalf of the United States of America, I declare the U.S. President has the power and will appoint Godly and wise people to offices that become vacant during the time period that the Senate is not in session.

In the name of Jesus Christ, on behalf of the United States of America, I declare the President shall only appoint those people to office for a short time as their terms expire at the end of the next Senate session.

§ SECTION 3: STATE OF THE UNION

1787 TRANSCRIPTION

He shall from time to time give to the Congress Information of the State of the Union, and recommend to their Consideration such Measures as he shall judge necessary and expedient; he may, on extraordinary Occasions, convene both Houses, or either of them, and in Case of Disagreement between them, with Respect to the Time of Adjournment, he may adjourn them to such Time as he shall think proper; he shall receive Ambassadors and other public Ministers; he shall take Care that the Laws be faithfully executed, and shall Commission all the Officers of the United States.

21ST CENTURY MODERN LANGUAGE

On occasion, the U.S. President shall tell Congress about the condition of the United States and the administration's plans for legislation.

The U.S. President shall recommend laws or other measures that he believes are necessary.

The U.S. President may call one or both Houses together if it is essential for the Houses to be in session.

The U.S. President may decide on the time to stop if the two Houses disagree about when to adjourn.

The U.S. President shall receive foreign ambassadors and other public officers.

The U.S. President shall make sure all the laws passed by Congress are carried out.

The U. S. President shall give instructions to the officers of the United States.

👑 KINGDOM DECLARATION™

In the name of Jesus Christ, on behalf of the United States of America, I declare the U.S. President shall tell Congress about the condition of the United States and the administration's plans for legislation.

In the name of Jesus Christ, on behalf of the United States of America, I declare the administration's plans for legislation will align with the Holy Scriptures.

In the name of Jesus Christ, on behalf of the United States of America, I declare the U.S. President shall recommend laws or other measures that he believes are necessary.

In the name of Jesus Christ, on behalf of the United States of America, I declare all laws or measures the President makes will reflect the heart of Jesus.

In the name of Jesus Christ, on behalf of the United States of America, I declare the U.S. President may call one or both Houses together if it is essential for the Houses to be in session.

In the name of Jesus Christ, on behalf of the United States of America, I declare the U.S. President may decide on the time to stop if the two Houses disagree about when to adjourn.

In the name of Jesus Christ, on behalf of the United States of America, I declare the U.S. President shall receive foreign ambassadors and other public officers.

In the name of Jesus Christ, on behalf of the United States of America, I declare the U.S. President shall make sure all the laws passed by Congress are carried out.

In the name of Jesus Christ, on behalf of the United States of America, I declare all laws passed by Congress will honor the U.S. Constitution.

In the name of Jesus Christ, on behalf of the United States of America, I declare the U. S. President shall give wise and Godly instructions to the officers of the United States.

§ Section 4: Disqualification

1787 Transcription

The President, Vice President and all civil Officers of the United States, shall be removed from Office on Impeachment for, and Conviction of, Treason, Bribery, or other high Crimes and Misdemeanors.

21st Century Modern Language

The U.S. President, Vice President, and all civil officers of the United States can be removed from office and impeached if convicted of any of the following crimes: treason, bribery, other high crimes, or misdemeanors.

Kingdom Declaration™

In the name of Jesus Christ, on behalf of the United States of America, I declare the President, Vice President, and all civil officers of the United States can be removed from office and impeached if convicted of any of the following crimes: treason, bribery, other high crimes, or misdemeanors.

In the name of Jesus Christ, on behalf of the United States of America, I declare our Presidents, Vice Presidents, and civil officers will not commit crimes, but be men and women of integrity.

§ SECTION 1: JUDICIAL POWERS

1787 TRANSCRIPTION

The judicial Power of the United States, shall be vested in one supreme Court, and in such inferior Courts as the Congress may from time to time ordain and establish. The Judges, both of the supreme and inferior Courts, shall hold their Offices during good Behaviour, and shall, at Stated Times, receive for their Services, a Compensation, which shall not be diminished during their Continuance in Office.

21st CENTURY MODERN LANGUAGE

The judicial power of the United States shall be held by the Supreme Court. There shall also be lower courts, that Congress can establish from time to time. The judges of the Supreme Court and lower court can serve as long as they maintain good behavior. The judges shall receive a salary for their work. The salary may not be reduced while they are in office.

Kingdom Declaration™

In the name of Jesus Christ, on behalf of the United States of America, I declare the judicial power of the United States shall be held by the Supreme Court.

In the name of Jesus Christ, on behalf of the United States of America, I declare there shall also be lower courts, that Congress can establish.

In the name of Jesus Christ, on behalf of the United States of America, I declare the judges of the Supreme Court and lower court can serve as long as they maintain good behavior.

In the name of Jesus Christ, on behalf of the United States of America, I declare all judges in all court rooms will be God-loving, Bible-believing, and honest.

In the name of Jesus Christ, on behalf of the United States of America, I declare the judges shall receive a salary for their work.

In the name of Jesus Christ, on behalf of the United States of America, I declare judges will be worthy of their wages.

In the name of Jesus Christ, on behalf of the United States of America, I declare a judge's salary may not be reduced while they are in office.

Declaring the U.S. Constitution

§ SECTION 2: TRIAL BY JURY

CLAUSE 1

1787 TRANSCRIPTION

The judicial Power shall extend to all Cases, in Law and Equity, arising under this Constitution, the Laws of the United States, and Treaties made, or which shall be made, under their Authority;—to all Cases affecting Ambassadors, other public Ministers and Consuls;—to all Cases of admiralty and maritime Jurisdiction;—to Controversies to which the United States shall be a Party;—to Controversies between two or more States;—between a State and Citizens of another State;—between Citizens of different States, —between Citizens of the same State claiming Lands under Grants of different States, and between a State, or the Citizens thereof, and foreign States, Citizens or Subjects. (Note: Clause 1 was modified by the 11th Amendment.)

21st Century Modern Language

The power the courts contain in the United States reach into the following areas:

Cases regarding law and equity that are covered by the U.S. Constitution, laws governing the United States, and its treaties.

All cases that will affect ambassadors, other public ministers, and consuls.

All cases of law concerning ships or the sea and other navigable waters.

All cases of law that extend to controversies between the United States and others.

All cases of law that extend to controversies between two or more States.

All cases of law that extend between a State and citizens of another State.

All cases of law that extend between citizens of two different States.

All cases of law that extend between citizens of the same State claiming lands under grants of different States.

All cases of law that extend between a State, or a citizen of a State.

All cases of law that extend between foreign States, citizens, or people.

(Note: Clause 1 was modified by the

11th Amendment.)

 KINGDOM DECLARATION™

Clause 1 was modified by the 11th Amendment. Please see Book 3 in the *Kingdom Declaration Series™* entitled, *Declaring Amendments 11-27*.

CLAUSE 2

 1787 TRANSCRIPTION

In all Cases affecting Ambassadors, other public Ministers and Consuls, and those in which a State shall be Party, the supreme Court shall have original Jurisdiction. In all the other Cases before mentioned, the supreme Court shall have appellate Jurisdiction, both as to Law and Fact, with such Exceptions, and under such Regulations as the Congress shall make.

 21ST CENTURY MODERN LANGUAGE

The Supreme Court is to try all cases that affect ambassadors, other public ministers, and consuls. The Supreme Court is to try those cases in which a U.S. State is bringing the case to court, or the State is being brought to court.

After decisions have been made in lower courts, the Supreme Court shall be a court to appeal to. Congress may make some exceptions or regulations to the appeal process.

 KINGDOM DECLARATION™

In the name of Jesus Christ, on behalf of the United States of America, I declare the Supreme Court is to try all cases that affect ambassadors, other public ministers, and consuls.

In the name of Jesus Christ, on behalf of the United States of America, I declare the Supreme Court is to try those cases in which a U.S. State is bringing the case to court, or the State is being brought to court.

In the name of Jesus Christ, on behalf of the United States of America, I declare after decisions have been made in lower courts, the Supreme Court shall be a court to appeal to.

In the name of Jesus Christ, on behalf of the United States of America, I declare Congress may make some exceptions or regulations to the appeal process.

In the name of Jesus Christ, on behalf of the United States of America, I declare Judges in the Supreme Court will be Godly men and women who will not pervert truth or justice.

CLAUSE 3

1787 TRANSCRIPTION

The Trial of all Crimes, except in Cases of Impeachment, shall be by Jury; and such Trial shall be held in the State where the said Crimes shall have been committed; but when not committed within any State, the Trial shall be at such Place or Places as the Congress may by Law have directed.

21ST CENTURY MODERN LANGUAGE

The trial of all crimes shall be by a jury. The exceptions are cases of impeachment. Trials shall be held in the U.S. State where the crime was committed. If the crime committed did not occur in any U.S. State then the trial shall be held at place Congress decides.

KINGDOM DECLARATION™

In the name of Jesus Christ, on behalf of the United States of America, I declare the trial of all crimes shall be by a fair and impartial jury.

In the name of Jesus Christ, on behalf of the United States of America, I declare trials shall be held in the U.S. State where the crime was committed.

In the name of Jesus Christ, on behalf of the United States of America, I declare if the crime committed did not occur in any U.S. State then the trial shall be held at place Congress decides.

§ SECTION 3: TREASON

CLAUSE 1

1787 TRANSCRIPTION

Treason against the United States, shall consist only in levying War against them, or in adhering to their Enemies, giving them Aid and Comfort. No Person shall be convicted of Treason unless on the Testimony of two Witnesses to the same overt Act, or on Confession in open Court.

21ST CENTURY MODERN LANGUAGE

Treason against the United States is war against the United States. Treason is the same as fighting on the side of our national enemies or giving assistance to the enemies of the United States. Nobody can be convicted of treason unless two witnesses can testify that the treasonous act was committed. A person can be convicted of treason if they confess in a courtroom setting in front of a judge and open public.

KINGDOM DECLARATION™

In the name of Jesus Christ, on behalf of the United States of America, I declare treason against the United States is war against the United States.

In the name of Jesus Christ, on behalf of the United States of America, I declare treason is the same as fighting on the side of our national enemies or giving assistance to the enemies of the United States.

In the name of Jesus Christ, on behalf of the United States of America, I declare people committing treason against our nation will be criminally charged, judged, and sentenced, to the fullest extent of the law.

In the name of Jesus Christ, on behalf of the United States of America, I declare nobody can be convicted of treason unless two witnesses can testify that the treasonous act was committed.

In the name of Jesus Christ, on behalf of the United States of America, I declare a person can be convicted of treason if they confess in a courtroom setting in front of a judge and open public.

Clause 2

 1787 Transcription

The Congress shall have Power to declare the Punishment of Treason, but no Attainder of Treason shall work Corruption of Blood, or Forfeiture except during the Life of the Person attainted.

 21st Century Modern Language

Congress shall have the power to determine the punishment for treason. Congress may not punish the family or heirs of a person convicted of treason.

Congress may only confiscate the property of a treasonous person during their lifetime.

 Kingdom Declaration™

In the name of Jesus Christ, on behalf of the United States of America, I declare Congress shall have the power to determine the punishment for treason.

In the name of Jesus Christ, on behalf of the United States of America, I declare Congress may not punish the family or heirs of a person convicted of treason.

In the name of Jesus Christ, on behalf of the United States of America, I declare Congress may only confiscate the property of a treasonous person during their lifetime.

Article 4

The States

§ SECTION 1: HONORING EACH STATE

1787 TRANSCRIPTION

Full Faith and Credit shall be given in each State to the public Acts, Records, and judicial Proceedings of every other State. And the Congress may by general Laws prescribe the Manner in which such Acts, Records and Proceedings shall be proved, and the Effect thereof.

21ST CENTURY MODERN LANGUAGE

Each U.S. State shall honor the laws, records, and court decisions of all the other U.S. States.

Congress can make laws to tell the way each State's laws, records, and court decisions shall be proved, and what affect they have.

KINGDOM DECLARATION™

In the name of Jesus Christ, on behalf of the United States of America, I declare each U.S. State shall honor the laws, records, and court decisions of all the other U.S. States.

In the name of Jesus Christ, on behalf of the United States of America, I declare Congress can make laws to tell the way each State's laws, records, and court decisions shall be proved, and what affect they have.

§ Section 2: State Citizens

Clause 1

 1787 Transcription

The Citizens of each State shall be entitled to all Privileges and Immunities of Citizens in the several States.

 21st Century Modern Language

The citizens of each U.S. State shall have the same privileges and protections as the citizens of all the States.

 Kingdom Declaration™

In the name of Jesus Christ, on behalf of the United States of America, I declare the citizens of each U.S. State shall have the same privileges and protections as the citizens of all the States.

Clause 2

1787 Transcription

A Person charged in any State with Treason, Felony, or other Crime, who shall flee from Justice, and be found in another State, shall on Demand of the executive Authority of the State from which he fled, be delivered up, to be removed to the State having Jurisdiction of the Crime.

21st Century Modern Language

A person who has been charged in a U.S. State with treason, a felony, or a serious crime and flees to a different State shall be brought back to the State where the crime was committed, especially if the governor demands it.

Kingdom Declaration™

In the name of Jesus Christ, on behalf of the United States of America, I declare a person who has been charged in a U.S. State with treason, a felony, or a serious crime and flees to a different State shall be brought back to the State where the crime was committed, especially if the governor demands it.

In the name of Jesus Christ, on behalf of the United States of America, I declare the people placed as State governors will be Bible-believing, Jesus-loving, and Holy Spirit-filled men and women.

CLAUSE 3

1787 TRANSCRIPTION

No Person held to Service or Labour in one State, under the Laws thereof, escaping into another, shall, in Consequence of any Law or Regulation therein, be discharged from such Service or Labour, but shall be delivered up on Claim of the Party to whom such Service or Labour may be due.

(Note: Slavery mentioned in the U.S. Constitution ended by Amendment 13.)

21ST CENTURY MODERN LANGUAGE

A person who is a slave in one U.S. State will not be free from slavery or bondage even if he escapes to another State. When he is caught in another U.S. State, he shall be sent back to the person who owns him or to the individual he owes labor to.

(Note: Slavery mentioned in the U.S. Constitution ended by Amendment 13.)

KINGDOM DECLARATION™

(Clause 3 was modified by the 13th Amendment. See Book 3 in the *Kingdom Declaration Series™: Declaring Amendments 11-27.*)

§ SECTION 3: NEW STATES

CLAUSE 1

1787 TRANSCRIPTION

New States may be admitted by the Congress into this Union; but no new State shall be formed or erected within the Jurisdiction of any other State; nor any State be formed by the Junction of two or more States, or Parts of States, without the Consent of the Legislatures of the States concerned as well as of the Congress.

21ST CENTURY MODERN LANGUAGE

Congress may admit new U.S. States into the Union.

Congress cannot create new States from part of another State.

Congress cannot join two States together, unless both the States and Congress agree.

Kingdom Declaration™

In the name of Jesus Christ, on behalf of the United States of America, I declare Congress may admit new U.S. States into the Union.

In the name of Jesus Christ, on behalf of the United States of America, I declare Congress cannot create new States from part of another State.

In the name of Jesus Christ, on behalf of the United States of America, I declare Congress cannot join two States together, unless both the States and Congress agree.

Clause 2

1787 Transcription

The Congress shall have Power to dispose of and make all needful Rules and Regulations respecting the Territory or other Property belonging to the United States; and nothing in this Constitution shall be so construed as to Prejudice any Claims of the United States, or of any particular State.

21ST CENTURY MODERN LANGUAGE

Congress has the power to make needed rules and regulations about territories and properties owned by the United States.

Nothing in this Constitution modifies the claims the United States has on its property, or any U.S. State has on its property.

KINGDOM DECLARATION™

In the name of Jesus Christ, on behalf of the United States of America, I declare Congress has the power to make needed rules and regulations about territories and properties owned by the United States.

In the name of Jesus Christ, on behalf of the United States of America, I declare nothing in this Constitution modifies the claims the United States has on its property, or on any U.S. State and its property.

§ Section 4: Republic Government

1787 Transcription

The United States shall guarantee to every State in this Union a Republican Form of Government, and shall protect each of them against Invasion; and on Application of the Legislature, or of the Executive (when the Legislature cannot be convened) against domestic Violence.

21st Century Modern Language

The United States guarantees that each U.S. State has a republic form of government.

The United States shall protect each U.S. State against enemy invasion. If a State's legislature asks for help against an invasion, the United States shall protect the State against violence within that State. If the legislature is unable to meet, then the State's governor can request protection.

👑 KINGDOM DECLARATION™

In the name of Jesus Christ, on behalf of the United States of America, I declare the United States guarantees that each U.S. State has a republic form of government.

In the name of Jesus Christ, on behalf of the United States of America, I declare the United States shall protect each U.S. State against enemy invasion.

In the name of Jesus Christ, on behalf of the United States of America, I declare if a State's legislature asks for help against an invasion, the United States shall protect the State against violence within that State.

In the name of Jesus Christ, on behalf of the United States of America, I declare if the legislature is unable to meet, then the State's governor can request protection.

Article 5

Amendment

1787 TRANSCRIPTION

The Congress, whenever two thirds of both Houses shall deem it necessary, shall propose Amendments to this Constitution, or, on the Application of the Legislatures of two thirds of the several States, shall call a Convention for proposing Amendments, which, in either Case, shall be valid to all Intents and Purposes, as Part of this Constitution, when ratified by the Legislatures of three fourths of the several States, or by Conventions in three fourths thereof, as the one or the other Mode of Ratification may be proposed by the Congress; Provided that no Amendment which may be made prior to the Year One thousand eight hundred and eight shall in any Manner affect the first and fourth Clauses in the Ninth section of the first article and that no State, without its Consent, shall be deprived of its equal Suffrage in the Senate.

21st Century Modern Language

The Constitution can be changed or amended when two thirds of both Houses of Congress find it necessary to modify or add to the Constitution. If modifications are deemed necessary, Congress shall write an amendment. A copy of the amendment shall be sent to each U.S. State. The States can assemble conventions to review the amendment and take a vote.

If three fourths of the States agree on the amendment, then it shall be added to this Constitution.

A second way to make amendments to this Constitution is when two thirds of the State's legislatures ask Congress to assemble a convention for requesting amendments.

Any amendment made by the convention must then be made official by a vote of three fourths of all the States.

Here is an exception:

There cannot be an amendment before 1808 that changes Clauses 1 and 4 in Article 1, Section 9.

Also, no U.S. State can lose their right to have an equal number of votes in the Senate.

KINGDOM DECLARATION™

In the name of Jesus Christ, on behalf of the United States of America, I declare the Constitution can be changed or amended when two thirds of both Houses of Congress find it necessary to modify or add to the Constitution.

In the name of Jesus Christ, on behalf of the United States of America, I declare if modifications are deemed necessary, Congress shall write an amendment.

In the name of Jesus Christ, on behalf of the United States of America, I declare a copy of the amendment shall be sent to each U.S. State.

In the name of Jesus Christ, on behalf of the United States of America, I declare the States can assemble conventions to review the amendment and take a vote.

In the name of Jesus Christ, on behalf of the United States of America, I declare if three fourths of the States agree on the amendment, then it shall be added to the Constitution.

In the name of Jesus Christ, on behalf of the United States of America, I declare another way to make amendments is when two thirds of State's legislatures ask Congress to assemble a convention for requesting amendments.

In the name of Jesus Christ, on behalf of the United States of America, I declare any and all proposed amendments will reflect heaven and God's perfect plan.

In the name of Jesus Christ, on behalf of the United States of America, I declare any amendment made by the convention must then be made official by a vote of three fourths of all the States.

In the name of Jesus Christ, on behalf of the United States of America, I declare no U.S. State can lose their right to have an equal number of votes in the Senate.

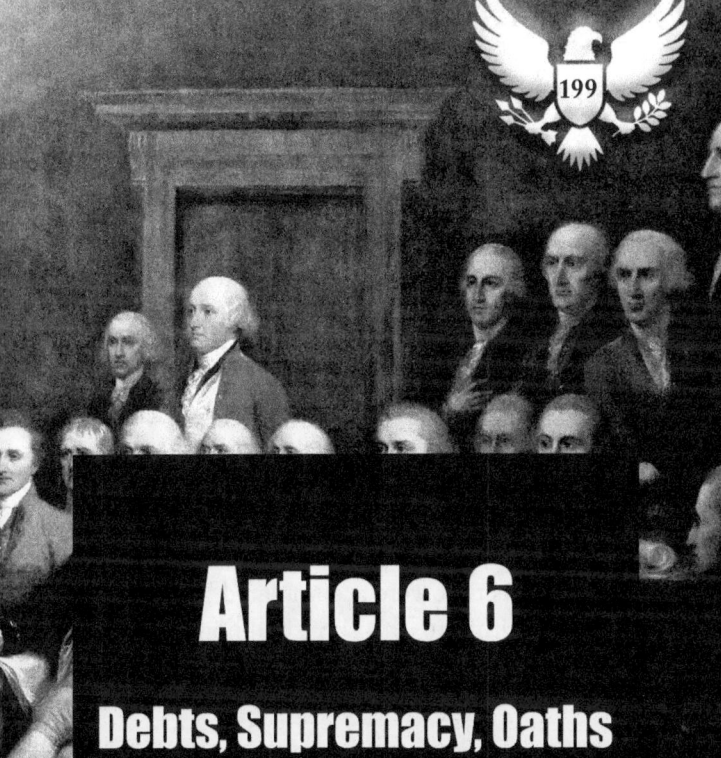

Article 6
Debts, Supremacy, Oaths

Clause 1

 1787 Transcription

All Debts contracted and Engagements entered into, before the Adoption of this Constitution, shall be as valid against the United States under this Constitution, as under the Confederation.

 21st Century Modern Language

The United States is still obligated to pay debts that were accumulated before this Constitution. The U.S. shall honor the commitments that were agreed upon under the Articles of Confederation.

 Kingdom Declaration™

In the name of Jesus Christ, on behalf of the United States of America, I declare the United States is obligated to pay debts that were accumulated before this Constitution.

In the name of Jesus Christ, on behalf of the United States of America, I declare the U.S. shall honor the commitments that were agreed upon under the Articles of Confederation.

CLAUSE 2

1787 TRANSCRIPTION

This Constitution, and the Laws of the United States which shall be made in Pursuance thereof; and all Treaties made, or which shall be made, under the Authority of the United States, shall be the supreme Law of the Land; and the Judges in every State shall be bound thereby, any Thing in the Constitution or Laws of any State to the Contrary notwithstanding.

21ST CENTURY MODERN LANGUAGE

This Constitution, the laws that are made according to it, and all treaties made under it shall be the supreme law of the land.

The judges in all U.S. States shall use this Constitution as their guide when they make decisions, no matter what it might say in the laws of any State.

Kingdom Declaration™

In the name of Jesus Christ, on behalf of the United States of America, I declare the Constitution, the laws that are made according to it, and all treaties made under it shall be the supreme law of the land.

In the name of Jesus Christ, on behalf of the United States of America, I declare the judges in all U.S. States shall use this Constitution as their guide when they make decisions, no matter what it might say in the laws of any State.

In the name of Jesus Christ, on behalf of the United States of America, I declare evil judges corrupting justice will be removed, charged, and sentenced to the fullest extent of the law.

In the name of Jesus Christ, on behalf of the United States of America, I declare there will be a holiness from God that touches each judge.

Clause 3

1787 Transcription

The Senators and Representatives before mentioned, and the Members of the several State Legislatures, and all executive and judicial Officers, both of the United States and of the several States, shall be bound by Oath or Affirmation, to support this Constitution; but no religious Test shall ever be required as a Qualification to any Office or public Trust under the United States.

21st Century Modern Language

The Senators, Representatives, members of State legislation, and all executive and judicial officers of the United States and individual U.S. States shall solemnly swear to support this Constitution. However, there shall never be a religious requirement for any office or public trust under the United States.

KINGDOM DECLARATION™

In the name of Jesus Christ, on behalf of the United States of America, I declare the Senators, Representatives, members of State legislation, and all executive and judicial officers of the United States and individual U.S. States shall solemnly swear to support this Constitution.

In the name of Jesus Christ, on behalf of the United States of America, I declare all elected officials will indeed support the U.S. Constitution.

In the name of Jesus Christ, on behalf of the United States of America, I declare there shall never be a religious requirement for any office or public trust under the United States.

In the name of Jesus Christ, on behalf of the United States of America, I declare even if religious requirements are not required for an elected official, those who are elected will be lovers of Jesus Christ and hold a morality found in the Holy Bible.

1787 Transcription

The Ratification of the Conventions of nine States, shall be sufficient for the Establishment of this Constitution between the States so ratifying the Same. Done in Convention by the Unanimous Consent of the States present the Seventeenth Day of September in the Year of our Lord one thousand seven hundred and Eighty seven and of the Independence of the United States of America the Twelfth In witness whereof We have hereunto subscribed our Names,

 21st Century Modern Language

When nine States approve of the Constitution in their conventions, then this Constitution shall be set up as the government for the States that have approved it.

This Constitution was created in this convention with the agreement of all of the States. We were present on the 17th day of September, 1787. It is the twelfth year of the Independence of the United States of America when we have signed our names.

KINGDOM DECLARATION™

In the name of Jesus Christ, on behalf of the United States of America, I declare when nine States approve of the Constitution in their conventions, then this Constitution shall be set up as the government for the States that have approved it.

In the name of Jesus Christ, on behalf of the United States of America, I declare the Constitution was created with the agreement of all of the States.

Signatories

211

1787 Transcription

GO WASHINGTON—President.
and deputy from Virginia

[Signed also by the deputies of twelve States.]

Delaware
Geo: Read, Gunning Bedford jun
John Dickinson, Richard Bassett
Jaco: Broom
Maryland
James MCHenry,
Dan of ST ThoS. Jenifer
DanL Carroll.
Virginia
John Blair, James Madison Jr.
North Carolina
WM Blount, RichD. Dobbs Spaight.
Hu Williamson
South Carolina
J. Rutledge,
Charles I.A. Cotesworth Pinckney
Charles Pinckney, Pierce Butler.
Georgia
William Few, Abr Baldwin
New Hampshire
John Langdon, Nicholas Gilman

Massachusetts
Nathaniel Gorham, Rufus King
Connecticut
WM. SamL. Johnson, Roger Sherman
New York
Alexander Hamilton
New Jersey
Wil: Livingston, David Brearley.
WM. Paterson, Jona: Dayton
Pennsylvania
B Franklin, Thomas Mifflin
RobT Morris, Geo. Clymer
ThoS. FitzSimons, Jared Ingersoll
James Wilson, Gouv Morris
Witness: William Jackson, Secretary

21ST CENTURY MODERN LANGUAGE

We sign our names as witnesses:

George WASHINGTON, President and delegate from Virginia

Delaware

George Read, Gunning Bedford Jr.

John Dickinson, Richard Bassett

Jacob Broom

Maryland

James MCHenry

Dan of ST ThoS. Jenifer

Daniel Carroll.

Virginia

John Blair, James Madison Jr.

North Carolina

William Blount, Hugh Williamson

Rich D. Dobbs Spaight.

South Carolina

J. Rutledge

Charles I.A. Cotesworth Pinckney

Charles Pinckney, Pierce Butler.

Georgia

William Few, Abraham Baldwin

New Hampshire

John Langdon, Nicholas Gilman

Massachusetts
Nathaniel Gorham, Rufus King
Connecticut
William Samuel Johnson
Roger Sherman
New York
Alexander Hamilton
New Jersey
William Livingston, David Brearley.
William. Paterson, Jona: Dayton
Pennsylvania
B. Franklin, Thomas Mifflin
Robert T. Morris, George Clymer
Thomas. FitzSimons
Jared Ingersoll, James Wilson.
Gouveneur Morris
Witness: William Jackson, Secretary

About Nathan D. Pietsch

Nathan D. Pietsch was born in Orange County in Fullerton, California,

on September 27th, 1976. As an infant, he was diagnosed with neurofibromatosis, a disease in which tumors attack the nervous system. His doctors anticipated a childhood death. However, the Lord healed Nathan miraculously. He is now a crusade evangelist, preacher, missionary, author, world traveler, and passionate follower of Jesus Christ.

Nathan and his wife, Dawn, travel the world preaching the Good News of Jesus Christ. They have helped bring freedom and transformation to thousands of people bound by the snares of the devil. It is their desire to see captives set free.

As frontline ministers, Nathan and Dawn have a heart for worldwide revival. They partner with churches around the globe to help release a great outpouring of the Holy Spirit in the regions they minister.

As a result, the churches grow in strength and number, unity is established, and the people are released into their life's purpose. Nathan and Dawn help bring renewal through: 1) Gospel crusade evangelism, 2) conducting training and equipping seminars, workshops, and conferences, 3) ministering deliverance and inner healing, and 4) clearing the land and territories of demonic principalities.

Nathan has written numerous books and is the author of the instant classics *The Holiday Devotional Series*. He has also written *Go: Testimonies from the Front Lines*, *Your Royal Destiny: Discovering Your Significance*, and *Decay Castle*.

Additional Resources at BattleAxeTV.com

Battle Axe TV is a media ministry of All Sufficient God Church. The website contains video recordings, audio recordings,

and written materials associated with Nathan D. Pietsch and ministry associates. As you watch, listen, or read, expect to receive healing, deliverance, encouragement, revelation, empowerment, equipping, impartation, or salvation.

At Battle Axe TV, we are training warriors for the Great Harvest. Jesus said in John 4:35c (NKJV), *"...Behold, I say to you, lift up your eyes and look at the fields, for they are already white for harvest!"* The great harvest of souls is upon us. God wants to use you to be a "fisher of men" to draw people to Himself. Battle Axe TV can help you prepare for your ministry call.

BATTLEAXETV.COM

Additional Books in the Series

DECLARING THE U.S. CONSTITUTION

We are living in unprecedented times. The rights and freedoms American citizens have enjoyed for generations are under attack. The foundation of our nation is being shaken. The U.S. Constitution has been trampled and spit upon. The blood of our forefathers who won us such privileges is being disgraced.

In *Declaring the U.S. Constitution* we will make *Kingdom Declarations™* that will help expel the darkness and bring transformation to the United States of America.

DECLARING THE BILL OF RIGHTS

America is at war. It is a war against light and dark, good and evil, bondage and freedom. It is a war between God's Kingdom and satan's domain.

In *Declaring the Bill of Rights* we will make *Kingdom Declarations*™ that will help expel the darkness and bring transformation to the United States of America.

DECLARING AMENDMENTS 11-27

Your voice is a *Warrior's War Trumpet*™ that destroys the works of the devil. Your voice sounds the alarm of danger. Your voice rallies the troops. Your voice carries fire. Your voice holds life and death.

In *Declaring Amendments 11-27* we will make *Kingdom Declarations*™ that will help expel the darkness and bring transformation to the United States of America.

Stay tuned for future release dates of additional books in the Kingdom Declaration Series™.

Connect with Nathan D. Pietsch

Battle Axe TV
www.BattleAxeTV.com

All Sufficient God Church
www.AllSufficientGod.org

Frontline Chronicles
www.FrontlineChronicles.com

Holiday Devotionals
www.HolidayDevotionals.com

Facebook
www.facebook.com/nathan.pietsch.9

Youtube
www.youtube.com/@battleaxetv1
www.youtube.com/user/AllSufficientGod

Amazon
www.amazon.com/author/ndp

Blogger
www.allsufficientgod.blogspot.com

Sow Into This Ministry

The ministry efforts of All Sufficient God Church are funded by donations and financial gifts from people like you. Every year, we see the lives of countless people impacted and transformed. By investing into All Sufficient God Church, you can be excited to know that you are a vital part of this process.

You can make a one-time donation, or become a monthly giver. Your generosity enables us to reach more people with the Good News of Jesus Christ. At the end of the year you will receive a tax-deductible receipt for your tax purposes. Thank you for your generosity and commitment to the Lord!

To sow a financial seed, please visit: www.AllSufficientGod.org/give.php

Schedule Nathan D. Pietsch

If you desire to schedule Nathan D. Pietsch for a speaking engagement you can contact All Sufficient God Church at:
www.AllSufficientGod.org

Nathan preaching in Kenya, Africa.

Nathan preaching in Oregon, USA.

Nathan preaching in Nigeria, Africa.

Nathan preaching in Washington, USA.

Forefathers' Blood

By Nathan D. Pietsch

Our forefathers' blood is being disgraced.
It is up to us to not let their sacrifice be erased.

Our forefathers were farmers who became patriots.
They did not anticipate their hopes of freedom spawning hate riots.

Our forefathers fought and died for freedom's sake.
The women watched their loved ones go with deep heartache.

Our forefathers overcame tyranny for America's sake.
They knew such evil must break.

Our forefathers battled against oppression that kept them bound
So yours and my liberty could be found.

Our forefathers fought and died to lose the bonds of wickedness.
They did not see future generations full of fickleness.

Our forefathers shook free of the heavy burden.
They knew they had to obtain victory, that's for certain.

Our forefathers overcame the oppressors to be free.
They had a dream of God's glory spreading from sea to shining sea.

Our forefathers suffered under an overwhelming yoke
To avoid our nation falling to the Ideology of Woke.

Our forefathers envisioned a land of the free and the home of the brave.
Let us not let their vision rot in the grave.

Our forefathers paid a great sacrifice.
To forget their legacy will not suffice.

Our forefathers' blood is crying from the ground,
"Don't lose this liberty we have found!"

Our forefathers fought and died in miry mud.
We must remember our forefathers' blood.

Get Right With God

Jesus is knocking at the door of your heart. He wants to empower, heal, deliver, and save you. If you desire to answer the call of Jesus and step into your true God-given destiny, please say the following prayer with sincerity of heart.

Jesus said, "Follow Me."

"Lord, I know that I have broken Your laws and commandments. I know I have fallen short of Your perfection. I am a sinner and in need of a Savior. Please forgive me of all my sins. Wash me clean in the blood of Jesus. I invite Jesus to become my Lord and Savior, to rule and reign in my heart from this day forward. Please baptize me with the Holy Spirit and fire. I receive all that You have for me. I pray all of this in the name of Jesus. Amen."

If this is the first time you have ever said this prayer, I want to welcome you into the family of God. You can now begin to fully experience the joy, peace, love, and power of the Heavenly Father, Jesus Christ, and Holy Spirit. We would love to hear from you and support you in your journey.

www.ingramcontent.com/pod-product-compliance
Lightning Source LLC
Chambersburg PA
CBHW071908290426
44110CB00013B/1325